Cooking with the Dead

St. Martin's Paperbacks Titles
by Elizabeth Zipern

COOKING WITH THE DEAD

100% DEAD (coming in 1996)

Cooking with the Dead

✳ ✳ ✳

Elizabeth Zipern

SMP

ST. MARTIN'S PAPERBACKS

This book has not been sponsored or endorsed in any way by the Grateful Dead.

To the many souls who have spent time on the road, Cooking with the Dead.

A portion of this book's proceeds will be donated to the Rex Foundation.

COOKING WITH THE DEAD

ISBN: 0-312-95483-2

Printed in the United States of America

St. Martin's Paperbacks edition/May 1995

10 9 8 7 6 5 4 3 2 1

❋ Acknowledgments ❋

This is a book about fans of the Grateful Dead. For this alone, the number of contributors is simply uncountable. Every individual present on the scene at one time or another has helped shape the society which has allowed so many of us to see the country, cooking all the way. Without help from so many Deadhead chefs, photographers, artists, and friends, during the fall of 1993 through the fall of 1994, this book would have never come to light.

But of course, the true authors are the food vendors who have spent some portion of their lives with the Grateful Dead. Immeasurable gratitude goes to all who took time out from yelling, cutting, deep frying, stirring, grilling and sautéing to be interviewed. By cooking up various culinary delights, they in their own ways are giving back to the Grateful Dead community.

I'd especially like to thank Bhakta, Jake and Lionel, Brian, Tom and the whole egg roll crew, Jonathan, Erin, Greg and Shea, Tim and Meredith, Shari, Pam and Jeremy, Andre, Rachel and Dupree for their help in all the parking lots we voyaged through together.

This project began with the guidance of Elizabeth Beier, was seen through by a great agent, Jim Trupin, and shaped by the most understanding and creative editor in the world, Jennifer Enderlin. Steve Silberman's advice and help were also priceless while learning about "the baptism of fire."

I would also like to thank some wonderful photographer friends, Raquel Heiny, Alec Bauer, Stephanie Siebert, Liz Schoenfeld and James "Lumpy" Crossman, all of whom gave advice, insight and great pictures. Visually, I am most indebted to a great photographer, printer, and friend, Mark Dablestein, who stayed up many a night to work on this because the information was really there. Jerry said so.

Help along the way came from friends at the *Tucson Weekly*, Beth Hawkins, Susan Knight, Royce Davenport, and Douglass Biggers. Also aiding was Deadhead sociologist Rebecca Adams, Roger Cohen, Dr. Barbara Reed, Gregg Morris, and, of course, the ever resourceful Internet. I thank my grammar-perfect mom for spending time editing and bringing moo-shu vegetables, as well as my dad, Andrew, and my favorite "best friend," Susan Rosenbaum.

Thanks to all the friends, contributors, critics, and wise ones who gave wonderful insight. I am ever grateful to the Bauers, Chris Beach, Stacy Breidenstein, Sandie Brodie, Lynn Brown, Amy Burtelow, CELA, Matt Cromey, James "Lumpy" Crossman, Pieter Voorhees and the George Street Co-op, Raquel "I wanna rock!" Heiny, Carol Jackson, KRAM, Jeff Lussen, Claudia Mari, Brian Merrick, Kevin Oakes, Soraya Rizek and Elijah James, Talia Rotblum, Samantha and Coal, Kristin Sawchuk, Liz Schoenfeld, Carmen Spiech, Kevin White, Alyson Witherspoon, oh . . . oh, and Kaya and Bear.

This list would surely be incomplete without the DOODES, many of whom volunteered to test out some of these recipes bringing their own insight and schnipps to help out: Kanad Chakrabarty, Alen Cileli, Larry Grodeska, Mike Nordstrom, John Pintar, Matt "Mass" Donohoe, Andy Gold, Kevin Gallagher, Candace Gyure, Steph Siebert, Laura Repetti, Scott "Scooter" Knect, Susie Stout, Sarah Malmstrom, Normandie Hilton, Andy Vota, Lori Lilly, Jen McCall, and everyone else I haven't mentioned.

Oh, and of course, thanks most of all, to the Grateful Dead, for the joy they have brought to so many is endless.

❋ Contents ❋

❋ Introduction ❋

When I close my eyes and try to remember, I can sometimes see the lighters flickering in the darkness. It was the second night of a three-show run at the Nassau Coliseum in '91 and I was thrilled to be back in the scene again. I had spent a magical second set creeping up and down hallways, hunting for an open space to dance, meeting a thousand and one souls along the way. By the time the set had ended, I hadn't been able to get enough of the intense delivery of emotion and energy the band gave off. I felt enchanted and illuminated that night, for the exuberant sound of Jerry Garcia's guitar still rolled around inside my head. I had fallen in love with a bunch of guys who were my parents' age.

The encore they played that night reminded me why I love the Grateful Dead. It felt like hours, waiting in the darkness, trying to predict the encore they were going to play. The moment they began the first majestic chords to "Lady with a Fan," effortlessly leading into "Terrapin Station," was electrifying. The crackling burst of energy left me speechless. Everyone began celebrating, roaring, hugging, smiling, and spinning as the story of Terrapin began to unfold. It was somewhere inside those first few notes that I first felt the immense exhilaration in my heart, a feeling that Terrapin always brings. In my own rotation I smiled a smile so wide it kind of hurt. The feeling of utter delight I had was almost metaphysical. I was home, and I knew it.

Many "Terrapins" and even more hallways later, I still get some of the same feelings when I'm inside a show. Since I began my "Grateful Deading" career, no music has rivaled the spiritual intensity nor the breathtaking joy that I have been lucky enough to find with the Grateful Dead.

One day I was thinking about the Dead's influence upon my life and the spiritual, physical, metaphysical, and emotional worlds they had shown me. On tour, I travelled all over the country. What other reason could I ever have to travel to Buckeye Lake in Ohio or to the illustrious Sam Boyd Silver Bowl in Las Vegas in the early summer? I must have been hungry, because I also started thinking about food. Back then I was, and still am, serious about eating consciously. On tour, I saw tremendous amounts of good, healthy food being prepared, sold and eaten. Though the population at-large may not know it, another world exists within the confines of the parking-lot area surrounding Dead shows. Here folks hang out, dance, vend, play guitar, drum their congos, play with babies, dogs, various toys, eat, and most intriguingly, they cook. Powered by generators, propane tanks, and solar panels, Deadheads manage to create a plethora of beautiful dishes at most any venue they travel to. From this on-the-road exposure to food I learned that a vegetarian diet consists of much more than pasta, bread and some veggies. I also became a conscious consumer, understanding where food comes from and the importance of staying away from the animal-based prepared processed junk that so many companies had been feeding America for years.

Increasingly, Dead shows have become a convention of chefs from around the country. The abundance of vegetarians (those who don't eat any meat, fish or poultry), vegans (those who eat no animal by-products at all), health nuts, and a smorgasbord of folks with different cooking backgrounds, makes for a complete education in parking lot cuisine. If I didn't love the Dead, I would have never come into contact with so many styles of cooking.

And so I began to gather recipes for these dishes that I saw. Since my own cooking style was rooted in the Dead scene, I was sure that other Deadheads had many of the same cooking experiences.

So I went back out on the road to find out what people were cooking. This book is a year-full of cuisine found in the parking lots of Dead shows. While researching, I went up to anyone and everyone and asked what they were making (and why they were following the Dead!). What I found were brilliant culinary creations. It was much better food than many Americans eat at home, considering a lot of vendors were cooking for dozens without even a measuring cup.

Try these recipes at home and make them with love, for as trite as it may sound, that is what they came from. Turn on some music, invite friends over to help, and enjoy yourself while you create. Don't be afraid to add, replace or take out ingredients; after all, it's your feast! Many of the ingredients can be found in health food stores or co-ops—important places for alternative eating and living. Get acquainted with your local co-op to discover another world in health and food.

These are Recipes from the Road. They are a reflection of the thousands of Dead fans who have vended, traveled to, and hung out at Grateful Dead shows since the band's inception in 1965. They also represent the marketplace and the society which lives on the road and cooks massive amounts of food to support an alternative lifestyle. The cooking makes a huge contribution to the scene, in a feast of the senses. At a show, food accounts for the myriad smells that emanate from the Shakedown (the parking lot "Main Street" where most of this food is sold). The familiar aroma of onions and garlic sautéing, and the sweet smell of cinnamon emanating from Fatty Egg Rolls, makes the scene feel like home. Combined with the mystical scents of burning sage and incense, it seems that to be a Deadhead is to immerse oneself in the smells, sights and music of the Dead, all the time, and to feel like you're always on tour. Happy Cooking!

Main Dishes

While tie-dye clad men and women hang out eating and listening to music in parking spaces next to him, Tom "Fried Rice" stands in the back of his commercial white truck in a mustard-and-oil stained shirt, deep-frying Fatty Egg Rolls into the night. Giants Stadium behind him roars in anticipation; the Dead are about to begin playing as the bright stadium lights shine high up into the sky, creating a ring of white light which blocks out all celestial bodies. "Looks like the show's about to start," he says glancing out of the back of the truck while turning the golden brown rolls over in the oil to cook on the other side.

It is the last show of the East-Coast tour; Giants Stadium, New Jersey, and probably the last place most of the vendors want to be. It is crowded, littered, and a far cry from many of the memorable scenic outdoor stadiums on the West Coast. But this last night, Tom and his crew of four are exhausted from working days that are sometimes fourteen hours long, cooking, prepping, and selling egg rolls.

"The egg roll thing is probably the most labor-intensive food on the whole entire lot. I think my crew is burnt out," Tom explains. But he also worries that if he and his crew didn't show up to the lot, there would be a lot of disappointed people. He's probably right. The smell of cinnamon used in the rolls wafting through the air, and the sight of people walking around with plum sauce and mustard dripping through their fingers as they lovingly devour the popular egg rolls is not uncommon.

Tom started making the egg rolls during the 1992 winter shows, and has since added some intense equipment. He has two deep fryers, a two-door commercial refrigerator, food processors, cutting boards, prep tables, egg roll bins, a plethora of plum sauce pumpers, mustard squirters, soy sauce sprayers, and an oven for "the special occasions."

Tom's egg roll days began like most vendors'. He wanted to go on tour but needed a way to make money while doing so. "I had a Volkswagen bus and two hundred dollars. I went out to Arizona for the winter '92 shows," he says. "With the two hundred dollars, I bought a fryer and propane tank, some vegetables, egg roll wraps and I started. I worked really hard."

To figure out what type of egg rolls would sell well on tour, he visited every Chinese restaurant that he came across. "I just kinda took the best of each recipe while keeping it vegetarian," he explains. "Poking around in my VW bus, stopping at all these little obscure Chinese restaurants. It's great, because it's the perfect excuse to stop at a restaurant and get good food."

Between tours Tom floats between Vermont and Santa Cruz, California, practicing Tai Chi and resting. He also holds a degree in biology with a specialty in molecular genetics from the University of Vermont, something that has helped him organize the egg roll enterprise.

Fatty Egg Rolls
(makes 20 or so fat egg rolls)

5-1/2 to 6 cups celery, chopped fine

5-1/2 to 6 cups (1/3 of a head) green or red cabbage (or both), shredded

6 cups (or 18) carrots, shredded

2 cups bean sprouts

Cinnamon or Chinese 5 spice, to taste, but use lots!

Vegan egg roll wraps ("Get good wraps, that's key," says Tom.)

Soybean oil (He doesn't use hydrogenated oil.)

Mix ingredients in a bowl. Place the veggies in the center of the egg roll wrap (follow rolling instructions on egg roll packages). Don't let the egg roll wraps get dry, or they will not wrap well. Keep them covered and use a spray bottle with water and a little oil to moisten each wrap before the veggies are added. Roll up (Tom rolls them into squares) but roll tight so the oil doesn't get in as much. Heat the oil to 375–400 degrees. Deep fry for a few minutes on each side. The inside will be lightly cooked, but still crunchy, and the wrap outside will be crispy and flaky.

STONER WARNING FROM TOM: "You've got to give stoners a warning," he says. "If you space off and leave the hot oil bath going while you're smoking out, it can catch fire. Be careful." The moral of the story: "Don't cook and smoke pot."

Fat sauces are key! Try hoisin, duck, soy, mustard or Teriyaki sauces.

"That's kinda what has enabled me to have a Fatty Egg Roll kitchen," he says. "You realize that it's not a big mystery to make it work. Develop a formula that works, and if it's not working then evaluate the formula and modify the formula.

"The fun part of the story is that, here's this guy who's working with radio isotopes in DNA and protein, and carrying out all these funky DNA extractions, and now he's, like, making egg rolls at a Grateful Dead parking lot!"

3

In the middle of cooking, Rasananda rests for a moment and walks around the parking lot. He has come to the Las Vegas shows to cook Samosas, a classic Krishna dish that he is known for. "When you think of Samosas, you think of Rasananda, and when you think of Rasananda, you think Samosa," says one fan.

Rasananda has come to yet another Grateful Dead parking lot to spread the word of Krishna. By selling the Samosas and small booklets on Krishna consciousness, he, and other followers of Krishna who have come to help, make their presence known. The group is usually hard to miss. For years, they've been on the scene wearing white-and-peach colored clothing, shaking tambourines, beating drums, and burning incense.

"I cook Samosas because I discovered three

Samosas
(should make 8–12)

"This Samosa can keep for three weeks outside a cooler," says Rasananda "You can make sweet Samosas or spicy ones. You can make Samosas with any kind of vegetables or you can use dahl."

FILLING
2 cups potatoes
1 cup cauliflower
1 cup peas
1/2 cup tomatoes
1 tsp. or more to taste of cumin, coriander, turmeric, curry, chili powder
Steam or boil the cauliflower and potatoes and then drain. Sauté them in oil with cumin, coriander, turmeric, curry, and chili powder. Add the tomatoes and peas. Mix well and continue to sauté until thick enough to stuff into the dough as a filling. When finished, take off heat, mix, and let cool.

DOUGH
2 cups white and/or whole wheat flour
Water—1/2–1 cup (or enough to make a dough)
1 tsp. salt
1/4 cup ghee (Ghee is butter which has had its protein solids cooked off. To make this, cook butter for a few hours over a low heat and scrape off the solids which form on the surface after cooking. To further separate the solids from the ghee, strain over a paper towel. Ghee can also be purchased in a co-op, health food store or Indian market.)

Mix the flour and salt with the ghee and add water to make a dough. Make equal golf-sized balls out of the dough and then roll flat with a rolling pin. Stuff the filling inside, then close tightly like a turnover for frying. Fry in oil combined with a few more teaspoons of ghee. Flip occasionally and fry until a light brown.

years ago when I came to America, that at Dead shows, people love the Samosa, especially in San Francisco," says Rasananda in broken English (he grew up in France). "I discovered that after the show, people love them so much. Now I make about 1,500 Samosas every show. Sometimes 2,000. Also, American people love potatoes. I realize that.

"I don't come just for the show. It's a good place because people like our food so much and they know that it is spiritual food, vegetarian, even vegan. They look for it. They know me, they look for me. Especially in Las Vegas. And it's a very good place for preaching for us," he explains. "Because we're not the kind of preachers that say, 'Oh, you're just demons!' We purify the people by chanting, by food, and by book. This food has a spiritual effect.

"Krishna is a name for God. It means the most attractive, and includes all the names for God. When we chant in the name of God, we become completely satisfied, free from fear we become peaceful. It is not a goal actually. The goal is to develop our love for God. In the scriptures—Bible, the Koran, Bhagavad-Gita—it says that we should chant in the name of God.

"We encourage people to chant the name of the god they like the most," he explains. "And if they have no name, they can chant the name of Krishna. They can realize the nature of the soul, God himself, and that we're full of knowledge, full of happiness, and we're eternal. By chanting the name, we want to chant more all the time and we become more and more happy. Our minds become clear, and Krishna is in the heart. Krishna says in the Bhagavad-Gita, 'Those who serve me with love and devotion I give intelligence by which they can come to me.' So only by love and devotion, can you understand Krishna. Otherwise we speculate for many lifetimes. And there's no other way, actually. There's only one religion. Our love for God. That's it. And this religion you're given, according to time and circumstances, just encourages people to raise their consciousness. It doesn't go against Krishna consciousness. Buddha just came to teach one thing about God, he didn't teach everything. By chanting and dancing and eating nicely, we look for happiness, but we do it in a spiritual way, and we get satisfaction."

Dead shows are known as a breeding ground for the politically inspired. Inside venues, groups like Greenpeace, Rainforest Action, and various Public Interest Research Groups set up tables and pass out literature to Dead fans. Outside the venues, political and social consciousness is dominant in the lots.

One of the spreading movements, in and outside of the Dead scene, is the campaign to reintroduce the use of hemp. People are becoming aware of the plant's multiple uses, other than just smoking it. Hemp plants are used for their fiber and oil. They are sustainable and a sturdy crop to grow. These oils and fibers are taken from the seeds and stalk of the plant. Hemp grown for biomass is worthless as an intoxicant. According to *The Emperor Wears No Clothes,* a prohemp book, hemp plants were one of the most harvested crops in the U.S. in the early 1990s. Believed to have been outlawed for political reasons, many activists are trying to bring it back for its positive environmental and medicinal effects.

Danbo has been a hemp activist since 1990. He first came in contact with the movement when he went to Los Angeles for a hemp rally. There he met hemp activists, including Jack Herer, author of *The Emperor Wears No Clothes,* the essential encyclopedia of the hemp story. Selling Hemp Falafel at Dead shows enables him to work in the Dead community, a culture that is very supportive of the issue.

"I organized some rallies down there to help spread the word, and after about two rallies, one of the people in our group said, 'Why don't we have a hemp-seed pancake breakfast?' " he explains. "That started the cooking with hemp seed. It was very successful. We made money for the group, and then from the pancakes we evolved into the burger, then we hit upon this falafel. This falafel is like the hottest thing going. People often say that everything they've tasted with hemp tastes so good, it just adds that special little flavoring that makes it mm, mm, mm!"

Danbo, his partner, Leah, and their son, Sativa, brought the hemp message to the Dead community, by making Dead Hemp Falafel at the Eugene, Oregon, shows in 1994. They knew that the Dead culture was hip to hemp. "Even if it touches one person, it's worth it for me to come down here and put in all the effort," Danbo explains. "I think our work is important here. And these are the people that care you know?

"I see hemp as not being the cure-all for everything, but it certainly can be a big step in the right direction. I believe hemp is more in balance with earth and nature itself. We're so far off, with the oil-based chemical petroleum society. It's killing us, there's no two ways about it. I have a lot of hope. We don't need to convince everybody, just a certain critical number.

"We're also talking about sovereign issues, and this is a very important part of the process to reclaim our inalienable rights we have from our creator," he explains. "We need to rethink about what exactly we have a right to. And as a sovereign, or state citizen, you're operating under common law.

"When we go back to the sovereignty issue and understand where that came from, we understand that it's not illegal," he maintains. "As a matter of fact, it's very much our right to do anything we want with this plant, as long as we're not harming anyone else, and that's very easy to do when you talk about no deaths reported from pure cannabis intake. I'm not interested in the right to smoke it. It wasn't till I found out about the other 50,000 uses that turned me onto it. People ask me if I put green stuff into this stuff. I'm not interested in getting people high, I'm just interested in serving them some really nutritious food. I think that when they see how good it is, they'll say, 'Yeah we do have a right, it's a good viable seed. We shouldn't have to subject ourselves to somebody else's laws when they are totally unconstitutional.'"

"They say, 'We'll give you the privilege of living here in the U. S. of A.' Well, it's not so pretty living here anymore, and we gotta wonder why. Thank God for hemp and all the other things that help. I think it opens a lot of people's minds to spirituality, and that's the beautiful thing about sovereignty anyway. You're answering to God, not people in the blue suits and ties."

Dead Hemp Seed Falafel
(serves 4–5)

Danbo says that this falafel can be eaten raw, and it makes a nice spread to dip pitas into. "The roughest thing with this falafel is finding pita bread that doesn't break apart when opened," says Danbo.

4 cups or 2 15 oz. cans garbonzo beans
6–8 sprigs parsley, minced
4–6 cloves fresh garlic, minced
1/4 cup fresh basil, minced
1/4 cup (or more) hemp seeds, roasted and
   ground fine. Hemp seeds can be ordered in
   bulk from the Ohio Hempery.
1 tsp. turmeric

1/4 cup margarine, softened
1 tsp. cayenne
Marjoram, to taste
1/2 tsp. black pepper, or more
1/2 cup cooked spelt or barley flakes
   (instead of wheat)
Coconut oil (for frying)
Pitas

In a bowl, mix the garbonzo beans together to turn them into a mushy consistency (or use a food processor).
Add parsley, basil, garlic; grind in hemp seed. Mix together along with spices: turmeric, marjoram, cayenne, pepper.
Mix it by hand. "Love it and say our mantras," says Danbo.
Let it sit one day before serving. Flavors blend nicely that way. Form into small balls or patties and sauté in coconut oil when ready to cook. Don't fry the falafel, just heat it!
Make a cucumber/lemon yogurt dressing.

CUCUMBER/LEMON/YOGURT DRESSING
1/4 cup plain yogurt
1/4 cup cucumber, diced small
2 tbs. fresh squeezed lemon or lemon juice
3 tbs. tahini

Mix well and add a little water to get a sauce consistency. Fill a pita with the falafel, top with the dressing and add lettuce & tomato if desired. Eat, and enjoy.

D o I like cooking?" Tracey Grismer asks her husband as she arranges a chunky piece of tomato onto a kabob skewer and he nods emphatically. "I cook big meals when my friends come over," says Tracey. "I'll cook for two to three hours to make dinner for everyone."

Usually she just makes burritos, but the vending scene at the 1994 spring shows in Phoenix was already inundated with dozens of assorted burrito vendors, so she opted for something different: grilled beef and chicken Kabobs Made With Love.

"With the beautiful weather, I thought we should barbecue," says twenty-four-year-old Grismer. "We were going to come out and grill our own food, and I figured I might as well try this."

Tracey, with the help of her sister-in-law, Alicia, vends because she enjoys meeting people as well as feeling like she's part of the show "It's your own way 'in' I guess," she explains.

Originally from Longmont, Colorado, Tracey waitresses in Tempe, Arizona, but says that she wants to travel and tour more. "The farthest we've traveled was to Vegas. We don't have the means to travel because our car won't make it. Where the car will make it is about as far as we go," she laughs. Her goal is to get a bus and take in the East Coast.

Why all this for a band? "You get hooked on the Dead," avows Tracey. "I think it's more because of the people than the music that makes shows great."

Kabobs Made With Love
(as many Kabobs you want to make)

Beef and chicken, cubed	Green peppers, diced chunky
Teriyaki sauce	
Soy sauce	Onion, diced chunky
Mushrooms, diced chunky	Tomatoes, diced chunky

Put soy sauce on chicken cubes, and teriyaki sauce on the beef. Put them and the vegetables on skewers. Grill on the barbecue for as long as you like.

There's nothing like that feeling right before you walk through the gates," says Deadhead Julia MacMillan. "You feel like you're just a cartoon character because you want to run and play so hard and you know you're just going to dance all night."

With ample excitement for the show, Julia and her friend, Becky, set out to go on the Dead's West Coast 1994 summer tour, along with nineteen friends from Colorado, Delaware, California, Seattle, and Florida.

"There is a core group of us that live in Colorado and we all know all these other people. It's either brothers or friends of friends that we went to college with. We all ended up getting together. It's kinda crazy, it gets kinda hectic. That's where the family thing comes in, everyone gets really close."

"Traveling with so many people, there's a lot of disagreements," she explains. "Like, 'We should go north, we should go south,' but that's with anything that is like a family. It is kinda hard to get motivated. If we had a bus and we were all together that would be easy, but we're in separate cars."

When not on tour, Julia and Becky live in Vail, Colorado, and work as waitresses. Living in a ski town allows them the freedom to leave for long periods of the summer.

"We have about six weeks where the restaurant is closed, and in those six weeks, I can leave," says Julia. "It's called mud season, no one is in Vail, and everything is dead. Everything melts and it's just all mud everywhere. It's a ghost town."

So they decided to go on tour and see the Dead. Julia says that she goes because of the ways it makes her feel. "It can be a lot of things," she explains. "It can be soothing to your soul if you're stressed, or it can be joyful excitement. It makes you move. There is no way that I could ever stand at a concert and not dance. You gotta move. It just all goes through your whole body and it's one of those things you hear, and you just can't let go."

While on tour, Julia and Becky sold 3 Bean Veggie Chili for the second year in a row. Though it was a vacation from her job, Julia says that vending on tour is work.

"I think touring is a lot of pressure. It's a lot of hustling, it's a lot of working and there's all sorts of pressures," she says. "There's a lot of thinking involved. It's not like you just pull in and throw everything on the lot and just sell and go. There's a lot of planning involved, you have to be organized, you have to know what you're doing. You have to feel out the situation, check out what's going on.

"Like here," she says referring to the lot in Seattle. "They're pretty harsh on vendors this year, so you gotta watch out for that. You don't want to get a ticket for vending without a license. There's a lot of planning involved, but I do it for the music.

"It's a sensory experience, being in the lot, hearing things, seeing things, talking to people, and of course there's the music. There's a lot of good food here, you get to taste a lot of things you probably never would have had before, and generally it's kind of like a family atmosphere, even with people you don't even know.

"It's kinda like being in a community. In your own community, and I know that people in the outside world have no idea what the hell it's all about, or why we do it, but there's so much involved. You don't just invest money here, you invest yourself. And what you invest, you get back. I've met more people who I probably would never have met if I had sat home in Colorado and never ventured out. That's the same way with everything I do, because there is so much to see hear, taste, and feel."

3 Bean Veggie Chili
(serves about 6–8)

1 can each of black, red, and kidney beans. (Julia likes to use kidney beans. She has found they hold up better because they're firmer.)
1 green pepper, diced
3 onions, diced
1 cup corn (to get the Southwestern flair)
2 28. oz cans whole peeled tomatoes ("I don't use sauce," she says. "They put a lot of sugar in it.")
1 12 oz. can tomato paste
1-1/2 tsp. (or more) cumin
3 tsps. chili powder
3 tsps. cayenne pepper
Salt and pepper—to taste
White pepper—to taste
5 or 6 medium cloves fresh garlic, minced
Olive oil

Sauté the spices, onion, and garlic in oil first, then add the rest of the vegetables. Add the remaining ingredients, bring to a boil, and let simmer for 4 to 5 hours to draw out the flavor of the spices. Add a little water if it gets too thick so it doesn't get heavy. It should have a nice consistency to it, like a soup, not like chowder. Continue to taste, adding spices when necessary.

"That's the way my mother makes her spaghetti sauce," says Julia. "It makes a nice thick chili. The longer you simmer it, the spicier it gets. A lot of times we'll try to prepare it before we even get to the show and just store it in containers, then reheat it. In every city we go to, we try to stay with a friend so we can take over their kitchen for a couple of hours, get everything prepped, and then be able to do it on the lot. It's cleaner, safer, and much more convenient."

Matt and Lisa Chamberlin can attest to the fact that bringing one child on tour is chaotic, but traveling with two children can be absolutely frenetic. Their friend Mike, dog Dylan, cat Bud, and daughters, Marley, a newborn, and Emily, age two, accompanied them on the 1994 summer West Coast tour, all in one motor home.

"When we did the West Coast with the kids, it was crazy," says Matt. "We had a huge motor home, and that made it a lot easier. I don't know if everybody could do this, to take kids on tour. It's just crazy. You've gotta be willing to work your ass off, but always have one eye on at least one of your children, not to mention the dog and the cat."

"The kids had an opportunity to hang out with their folks, when their folks are really happy and really comfortable with their life," adds Lisa. "Not a lot of kids get the opportunity to do that, and it really would make a difference. When they get older, they don't want to hang out with you. We get the opportunity now. I really think it's going to make a difference in the long run."

The shows at RFK in Washington, D.C., were a bit of a break for the group. Matt and Lisa dropped Marley and Emily off with their grandparents, so Matt, Lisa, and Mike had time to hang around the scene and sell Torchin' Hot Tuna Melts, known parking lot–wide for the way Matt cooks them. The cheese on top is melted by torching them.

"The second night at Cal Expo, we were running out of grilled cheese," explains Matt. "The people who we were hanging out with happened to have two big cans of tuna. I had the buns left over from sandwiches, and a bunch of extra cheese. So I said, 'Let's try a tuna melt!' with the thought that the way I would melt the cheese, was to grab my torch, screw it on to my tank and see how that worked. I lit it up, and rocked it out, and people absolutely loved watching the flame. Because it's an unregulated torch, it made a very large flame which drew in the attention. People laughed, my wife thought it was ridiculous, but before we knew it, we were sold out!

"Torchin' Tuna Melts!" he yells out as people walking by stare at the glowing yellow flame.

"It's a gas burner from a small grill with a couple of attachment pieces which hook it to a regulator. Then that goes down into a hose which goes to my tank," he says. "The way I did the regulator, it's not high pressured, so it gives a yellow flame which draws the eye a lot more than the blue flame would. Also, any kind of wind makes it flare up. It's pretty sick. I've only burned myself once, and that was today for the first time. I didn't burn it bad enough to even show at this point. Just hurt for an hour. I did the whole West Coast without singeing a hair. I burned a few other people," he jokes. "Free body burning!" he yells out to the lot, laughing.

Torchin' Hot Tuna Melts
serves 2

1 can dolphin free tuna fish
2-3 tbs. real mayonnaise
salt to Taste
1/4 tsp. garlic powder
1 tsp. mustard
2 shakes black pepper
Basil to taste
1/2 tsp. thyme - "The kick flavor," says Matt
Parsley to taste
1/4 tsp. dill
1/4 cup carrots, shredded
1/4 cup celery, chopped fine
2 English muffins
Cheese-Try romano, mozzarella, jack, white cheddar

Mix the ingredients together and serve on a toasted English Muffin. Add cheese on top and put in the toaster oven or broiler to melt the cheese. Top with chives.

13

Sacramento in the summer is a hot place. Fifty miles east of temperate San Francisco, dry yellow grasses wave in the hot wind when temperatures soar into the high nineties. At the Sacramento venue, Cal Expo, the first venue on the Dead's 1994 West Coast tour, the temperature is affecting vending in the lots.

Silvana DiFranco and Dean Stubbings can't take out the homemade candles they've made until nighttime. The hot air is so stifling, they'd surely melt. So the two focus their energies on selling homemade Guacamole and Salsa with Chips, the first of many dishes they are vending throughout the West-Coast tour.

They conceived the idea to make guacamole when Dean was working as a handyman at a South American restaurant. "They have food from all over South America," Silvana says. "I'd never seen guacamole and salsa at shows, and we thought maybe it'd be a different idea."

After years of practice, Silvana loves to vend at shows, especially food. "It's a great way to show off your talents in arts and crafts, and your culinary skills in vegetarian and vegan foods," she says. "It's also satisfying to know you've fed someone a good, wholesome dish. Plus it pays for your gas, tickets and travel expenses. Nitrous Oxide, on the other hand, trashes the lot and the whole concept of vending, because it's all about money, and when it's all about money, it doesn't belong in a Grateful Dead parking lot."

Fresh Salsa, Guacamole
(serves 2–4)

GUACAMOLE
3 avocados
Lemon juice
Cilantro, minced

Onions, diced small
A little garlic, minced
Tortilla chips

Dean and Silvana don't measure amounts when they make their Guacamole and Salsa. "It's all up to individual taste," says Silvana. "I think it works better that way." Mix together all the ingredients but add the lemon juice at the end, or else its acidity will taint the taste.

HOMEMADE SALSA
3 plum tomatoes, diced
3 regular tomatoes, diced
1 small onion, diced

Cilantro, minced
Garlic, minced

According to Silvana, the salsa should be fresh and juicy. "Not like a cold tomato sauce," says Silvana. "Let the pulp of the tomato create its own salsa." Mix together and enjoy.

14

Silvana has been making candles since 1991, and has found that they sell well on tour. Along with homemade crafts like wood carvings, clay beads, bowls, and jewelry, home-created candles at shows are common, but are sometimes hard to find, especially in the summer when they can easily melt.

"They're extremely unusual because we never bought candle molds," she says. "We just took office supplies, like little square pencil holders and Tupperware shapes. I haven't seen any candles like them. We do mostly earth tones, Aztec colors, indigenous Indian colors, but we also have a lot of purples and pinks. We took the cheapest and the most inventive way out. They're really nice. I would like to pull them out later tonight, but it's too hot," she laments.

Dean and Silvana just moved to Berkeley where they plan on going to more shows to see the Dead and be with their tour "family."

"There is just not enough romance left in this nation anymore," Silvana explains. "Music fills that void, music as a universal language, per se. The Grateful Dead just happen to speak our tongue. Combine the beauty of the music, along with the kindness of friends and family we travel with, and you get a wonderful, rich flavor of life, love, and adventure. A recipe everyone should follow for at least a summer."

Throughout the winter and early spring months, many a Deadhead has caught and passed the perpetually circulating tour cold. During cold weather tours, Deadheads on the road typically don't eat right, nor do they get enough sleep. Sharing food, drink, and smoke, doesn't help either. The "always sick on tour" scenario is an affliction that Deadhead Andre Cantelmo was tired of dealing with, so he did something to change his eating habits. He started making Good Lovin' Lentil Soup.

"I would go on tour and get run down and sick a lot," he explains. "After a while I realized I wasn't eating right. There's only so much grilled cheese that you can eat. That's the main staple of tour. People eat grilled cheese day in and day out, I mean it's just not good enough.

"During the fall and spring tours, it would get real cold, which would increase the chance of getting sick, so I started making my own stews. My batches of stew kept getting bigger because people would smell it and they would want some.

Good Lovin' Lentil Soup
(serves 6–8)

"Stews are hearty, warm, good for your belly, and good for your head," says Andre.

3 cups lentils
14 cups water (or vegetable stock, though water works fine)
15 oz. tomato sauce
6 potatoes, diced
12 carrot sticks, diced
1/2 stalk celery, diced
3 onions, diced
10 to 15 garlic cloves, minced
Basil, black pepper, oregano, dill weed, parsley, thyme, rosemary—tarragon optional ("Have a personal party with these spices," says Andre.)

Dice the vegetables small enough so that at least three different veggies are represented on your spoon at one time. Leave the skins on. This helps to keep the flavor in.

Put the water in a pot, throw in lentils, spices, and the tomato sauce. Stir and bring to a boil. Turn down to a low simmer and let stew for three hours.

Add the vegetables and let stew for another hour. According to Andre, spicing this dish is a careful process. "For the spices, make a cup with your left hand and pour the spice into your hand. When the spice fills the cup of your hand and overlaps your life line, you have precisely the amount of spicing you'll need for this dish. Do the same for each spice. But add only a pinch of thyme."

It will then be ready to serve. Andre suggests you prepare it the day before the show, for it tastes best that way.

When it's cold, you really need good food to keep going and to bring your energy levels back up because all that dancing really adds up. It seemed like a good way to make money for gas and tickets, but it was also serving something wholesome and cheap. It was giving back to the community I belonged to."

Andre remembers going to his first Dead show in 1983 at Madison Square Garden when they played with Steven Stills. Since then he has seen over fifty shows and loves to introduce new Deadheads to the scene.

"New people are it!" he exclaims. "I think the most important thing is taking people to their first Dead show and the realizations they then make. A lot of people don't understand the sense of community that goes on there. Most people are not used to such a large number of people coming together and not only getting along without conflict, but honestly trying to positively contribute to each other's life experiences. Even if it's just for the six hours from when you show up at the lot to when you leave the lot.

"I recently took one of my friends to her first show, the 1994 Giants Stadium show with Traffic. And her remark was, 'Why didn't anybody tell me about this?' She was like, 'Everybody is so beautiful!' We never even bothered to try to get tickets, or score a miracle. She was completely infatuated with what was going on in the parking lot. One of the more epic scenes that impressed her was the disco party in lot 4G, next to the Shakedown. My friend was so happy to be dancing in the middle of a parking lot with two to three hundred other people, all of whom had been shut out of the show that night, but refused to stop having a good time."

"Those are the most important experiences that the Dead bring to us, not necessarily to get into the shows or commune with the band. The Dead bring us together into a funkadelic space of our own and sharing that space with each other is what the scene is all about for me. The Dead provide a way fat groove."

17

One of the best parts about going to a show, is meeting the pets that people bring to the scene. Cats, dogs, snakes, birds, and even roosters have been known to accompany their owners into the lot, with the unusual ones getting ample amounts of attention, for it's not every day that you see a rainbow-colored chicken pecking at the ground in a parking lot. (It happened at the '94 shows in Eugene!)

And then there are the dogs. Of all ages, shapes, and sizes, they accompany their owners into the parking lots, at times roaming about with their own agenda. These animals know what it's like to be on tour. They are Deadheads in their own way.

Merlin is a huge, shaggy, black, part–English sheepdog, part-lab with a big, gray face and huge paws. He is twelve years old, 100 pounds, and has been on tour since 1989. Merlin knows his way around most any parking lot his owners go to. He has his own friends.

"My dog has gone to all the shows that I've gone to," claims his owner, Todd Van Vactor. "There are lots of people who don't know me, but they know my dog. He's got a big old gray face, people come out of the show, and they go, 'That dog looks

9 Veggie Stir Fry
(serves 4–6)

All the vegetables should be added in equal parts (except green onion)

1/2 cup broccoli, diced
1/2 cup carrots, sliced
1/2 cup zucchini/squash, sliced
1/2 cup cabbage, sliced thin
1/2 cup mushrooms, sliced
1/2 cup green peppers, diced

1/2 cup green onion, chopped fine
1/2 cup bean sprouts
1/2 cup snow peas
Sauce
Red chili garlic sauce
Soy sauce
Canola oil
2 cups rice, raw

To start out, the wok should be really hot and should stay hot without burning the vegetables or oil. Start the rice and begin to saute the vegetables in canola oil. Cook the heavier vegetables first (in the order listed) for a minute or two before adding the lighter ones. The whole process should take about 4-5 minutes.

Make yourself your own secret stir fry sauce. Try different seasonings and sauces to taste. Todd's is a little hot, spicy, and/or sweet. Add this before you begin to stir fry, or as a sauce after. Serve over rice.

18

like Jerry!' " He laughs. "It's pretty funny.

"They did a little article in the Indianapolis paper about my tie-dye business, Spectral Enterprises, and when they came out to do the photograph, Merlin was in the shot with us. Everybody knows this dog. He's an old timer."

Todd and Merlin sell 9 Veggie Stir Fry and tie-dyed T-shirts to support themselves while on tour. Todd attributes his vending success to producing a quality product which Deadheads can rely on.

"There are a lot of vegetarians on tour that I see over and over again," Todd says. "They know what they're getting when they get my stir fry. And that's because I do give a lot to people.

"I pretty much see the same people on tour; the tourheads that are vegetarian and know how to take care of themselves because they've been on the road long enough to know what to do. There's a lot of really good food out here, but you can also get bad food and get really sick if you're not careful. I think that's what my stir fry has going for it. You can see it out there in the containers, and it's fresh, and it's clean. You know up front what you're going to get.

"It's funny because there are all different kinds of people who come to the shows, and I think they come for all different reasons. I think some people like to come for the music, and I think some people come because they know they'll see all their friends here, and I think some people come because they like to party, and they know that this is the right place and time for that. Just a lot of different reasons. I probably fare a little bit of all those things. I like the music, I see my friends here, I like to party and have a good time."

From the back of their truck, Greg and his girlfriend, Erin, spend most of the daylight hours at the spring 1994 shows in Phoenix making and selling the sometimes legendary "Gilly Melt."

The Gilly Melt, similar to a folded quesedilla but with lots of vegetables inside, has its roots in Mexico, where Greg and Erin learned how to make the tortillas from their friend

Sandra. "If she knew that I was at a Grateful Dead show selling tortillas, she would flip," says Greg. "She makes tortillas for her family every day. This lady can just whip them out like it's nothing."

Greg's creation has helped them go on countless tours by paying for gas, tickets and a place to sleep. "Vending is how I survived on summer tour last year at Shoreline and Eugene," explains Greg. "I started out with five dollars and I came home with five dollars. I got into the show, got a lot of beer. The product sells well. People walk by and see me clopping tortillas, and they're all like, 'Wow! That brother there, he's doing it!' I wouldn't feel good about myself, buying tortillas, buying salsa, and just sitting it out here. Anybody can do that. It's not the joy of cooking. The joy of cooking is making everything and having someone sit down and just go, 'Mmmm.' "

Greg's creation is dubbed after his nickname, Gilly, which according to him is short for "Gilbert the frugal messiah who runs naked through corn fields." It was tagged by a friend when he and Erin were in high school. Now, Greg likes to use the name while he cooks, something he is remarkably passionate about.

"Here in America, people have lost the value of cooking, and that's one of the reasons why I want to be a chef," he says. "It's about time that everyone woke up, stopped eating fast food, and realized that we are what we eat, and what you put into something is what you get out of it, especially in our food. Everyone is running around with their head cut off saying, 'Our world is so crazy, so complex, what do I do?' It's simple. Just do your own part. Eat right. Choose the things that you want in your body."

Both Greg and Erin are vegetarians, as is their son, Shea, who was born two months after the Phoenix shows, in May. Greg says that he is struggling to eat vegan, but claims that he "gets caught up on pudding."

Now they cook for Shea with tomatoes, broccoli, cauliflower, and artichokes picked from their garden. Though Shea was at two shows (while Erin was pregnant) she hopes to bring him to a Dead show one day. "One of my goals, dreams, is to take my child to a Dead show or even a Jerry show, or a Crosby, Stills, and Nash show. Wherever I go, he goes!"

The Gilly Melt

(makes about 2 dozen tortillas or more, depending how you shape the tortilla)

The best thing about this recipe is that you make your own tortillas, which is great for vegetarians who want to stay away from animal products, but still eat great tortillas. "Most tortillas have calcium phosphate or calcium sulfate (which are ground up animal bones)," says Greg. "They have all these things with fancy names in your food now."

HOMEMADE TORTILLA

3 cups wheat or white flour
2 pinches salt
About 1 1/2 cups lukewarm to warmer water
2 globs vegetable shortening (Erin recommends that you scoop it out with your hand.)

GILLY MELT FILLING

Green onions, chopped fine
Cilantro, chopped fine
Monterey jack and cheddar cheese (Greg says to make sure that you use cheese that is made without rennet.)

SALSA

10 fresh romaine tomatoes from the garden, diced. This is the main ingredient.
2 white onions, diced
1 bundle cilantro, minced
1 cerrano pepper, finely chopped

Jalepeno pepper diced
1 yellow pepper, diced
1 tb. vinegar
1/2 tsp. salt

To make the tortilla, knead the dough until all the lumps are gone. Place in a bowl and lay a paper towel over it and let sit for about half an hour. If the dough is too sticky, add flour. Take about a tablespoon full of dough, and press it into a tortilla. Erin cautions that this takes *a lot* of practice, so keep rolling.

To make the Gilly Melt itself, lay the homemade tortilla out flat, add cheese, and let it melt in a frying pan. Add chopped cilantro and green onions and some salsa. Fold the tortilla over and cook in oil for about two minutes on each side. Add salsa.

For the salsa, Greg and Erin don't use the same measurements every time. They say it's all done by eye and by practice. So, combine the ingredients and let ferment by sitting for just one day.

Whenever Tom Larose and his wife Coco open a restaurant, they have a tradition. They go to a Dead show and celebrate by vending one of their favorite dishes. In 1994 when they opened their second restaurant in Nashua, New Hampshire, they traveled to the shows in Highgate, Vermont, to continue the custom.

"A few years back, we had opened the first store up in Coleburg when they played in Maine, and we just opened this one (in Nashua). So it was like, anytime we open a store they come and play close by," says Tom.

Tom's and Coco's restaurants are Vital Vittles in Coleburg, New Hampshire, and Larose's Vital Vittles Market in Nashua, where they specialize in vegetarian food and organic produce. "I think I've got the only vegetarian place in the state of New Hampshire, and it's just like avocado and sprout California kind of food," says Tom.

The family plans on opening another store, so that each of Tom and Coco's kids, Adam, Tahlia, and Jean-Phillipe will be able to work in them when they grow up.

"My family is in the restaurant business," Tom says. "They opened the modern restaurant in Nashua in the thirties. So when I came back to Nashua to open a second store, I had to make it a restaurant, too. I like to tell people that when my grandfather started in the thirties, he used all organic veggies. They hadn't started spraying everything yet.

"Even though we're vegetarians, we're more hyper about organic farming," he maintains. "We really think it's a shame that farmers who love the land have to spray the stuff because they think that's the only way that they can make a profit. It's not a good long-term vision. The whole point is, if people don't buy organic and help the farmers make a living, they'll be fewer of them. If it's a healthy industry with all the organic farmers saying, 'We did all

22

right,' a lot more people who want to go organic, will."

For the Highgate shows Tom and Coco prepared organic Mesclun Wraps, a fresh green salad mixed with other vegetables and wrapped in an organic tortilla. "We just figured that you don't see too many fresh veggie wraps," says Tom. "Fresh veggies are always stir-fries and burritos. We thought some good raw fruit and fresh sprouts is just what you need after abusing yourself."

Tom's first show was in 1972 in Connecticut. "I wasn't much of a Deadhead then," he admits. "I kinda knew The Band and the Allman Brothers more than the Dead. But then I went to see them a lot at the Music Hall in Boston, and by the late seventies and eighties, I was a regular."

"I've always loved the vending at shows and the food particularly," explains Tom. "There was always a lot of good vegetarian food at the Dead shows. Food brings people together. Everybody gets the same rush from olive oil and garlic, it's just one of those things that go together."

Mesclun Wrap
(serves 2)

Mesclun is an assortment of mixed greens, that change according to the time of year. "Basically it depends on whatever is coming out of the ground at the time," explains Tom. "They are little edible flowers, and different baby things, like baby Swiss chard, and baby purple runner beans." If the Mesclun mix is hard to find, look for dandelion greens, plantain greens, Johnny-jump-up flowers, wild greens, mint leaves, and other assorted greens. Tom's favorite is arugala.

Tom and Coco try to use all organic ingredients. They also grow many of their own vegetables, including sprouts. "Sprouting food really improves the nutritional profile, it really does help," says Tom. "Especially beans and things, instead of being gassy, it tends to turn them into a vegetable where they digest very well."

1/2 cup mesclun greens
2 organic sprouted wheat tortillas
2 slices of cheese
1 cucumber, sliced
1 tomato, sliced
1/4 cup sprouts, any kind
Apple cider vinegar, to taste
Safflower mayonnaise, to taste
1/4 cup carrots, finely shredded

In a tortilla, add the toppings, and sprinkle the apple cider vinegar over the mix. Roll up. Leave enough veggies to make the second wrap.

For those fortunate enough to live on the West Coast during the last thirty years, the opportunity to see a Dead show without traveling too far has always been available. As a result many California Deadheads are accustomed to seeing the Dead, as well as other notable acts who frequently play the Bay area.

At thirteen, Brayton Tipping began going to as many shows as he could get to. "I rode my bike to my first show," says Brayton. "It was at Irvine Meadows and I rode my bike through the hills and through these strawberry fields. We had a troop in high school. We were dedicated. We would ditch school on Friday, go to Oakland, Greek, and Frost, leave after the show on Sunday and make school by Monday morning."

Now, a religion and philosophy major at UC Davis, who studies agriculture on the side, Brayton doesn't get to catch quite as many shows, but says he will always go see them.

"Even when the Dead play like absolute crap, I'll still go," he says. "It's where all my friends are. My spirit family. The Dead is the only thing that is close to fantasyland anywhere. Magic. It's the chance to feel like you're eight years old, playing with your friends, forgetting about worries."

In the past, Brayton has financed his Grateful Dead touring escapades by selling T-shirts, beer, ginseng, baked goods, burritos, homemade juice, and even mulberry banana bread, as well as photos of the Dead. At the Oakland Chinese New Year shows in 1994, he and his friend Jerome sold Vegan Sushi.

"This stuff is a lot of work, and we could sell it for more," says Brayton. "But it's so nice to just style people with really healthy food."

Working as an organic farmer, Brayton revels in the chance to watch the "evolution from seed to plant to food" and likes to be conscious of where food originates. He grows medicinal herbs, fresh and dried flowers, tomatoes, corn, squash, peppers, basil, garlic, onions, beans, peas, watermelons, gourds, cantaloupes, and pumpkins. Brayton also volunteers at a teaching farm for kids. "We do tours for kids from kindergarten through second grade," he explains. "It's like a demonstration garden; it teaches biology using the farm. I love that."

For Brayton, going on tour is an experience which holds its own magic. "It's not to get to a place, it's the in-between part," he says. "I went to New York in September, and that is one of the grossest places in the world. But the shows there, the people, and the culture are far different. Back there are all types, Chicano Deadheads, Italian Deadheads. It's cool."

Though he has spent quite a bit of time on the road, Brayton cautions that the rigors of touring can be hard on the body. "It's such a hard life," he says. "You see a lot of people who are trying to live consciously and be kind but they're smoking cigarettes and eating whatever comes to them and not thinking about it. The rigors of the road are hard, and if you aren't set up with good people, things can go wrong. Fortunately, I've been doing it enough where people take care of me, even if I get down."

Ganesha's Vegan Sushi

(makes 4 sushi rolls)

4 sheets Nori seaweed	Tofu Marination
1 cup raw organic brown rice	Italian parsley
1–2 tbs. barley miso ("The barley miso is just an incredible live cultured food with wakmae [another type of seaweed]," he says.)	Apple cider
	Ginger
	Sake
	Rosemary
	Tamari
1 cup tofu, marinated	Brown rice vinegar
1 cup chard, dark leafy green, steamed	Garlic
	Toppings
1–2 carrots, sliced small and lengthwise	Fresh pickled ginger
	Wasabi

Next, cook the brown rice and let cool. Add the miso to the rice and mix well.

Take out the sheets of seaweed. On a bamboo rolling mat, lay the seaweed flat and fill rice along half of the seaweed (horizontally). Fill so that it covers all the seaweed in this area. In the middle of the rice, place the baked tofu slices, and other seasonal vegetables from the garden. (Brayton uses shredded chard, carrots, kale, and winter squash.)

Follow the same process for each of the four sheets.

Roll up by pressing the seaweed inward toward the filling with your thumbs. Keep doing this until you have a nice, tight roll. On top, add slices of fresh pickled ginger, a bit of wasabi, and then dip into tamari. Eat and enjoy!

Ever since people began taking fine cuisine on tour, they've known that successful cooking on the road requires organization and adaptation to small cooking spaces, minimal materials, and often a lack of water. Whether it's washing dishes, cutting vegetables, or cooking in the back of a truck, a kitchen-away-from-home set-up is crucial.

Shari Dell expanded on her capacity to cook well on the road a few years ago when she converted her '82 Chevy into a traveling kitchen of sorts, complete with double stove (her twelfth one), bakery racks, and cases of fresh vegetables.

"When I got this van, it was a plumbing vehicle," says Shari. "I redid the interior, laid the floor, and cut back the roof to make it into a conversion kitchen." In addition, she added a prep table, shelves, pressure cooker, and other amenities of a well-stocked kitchen.

At one time a cooking contributor in the infamous "Burrito People" crew, Shari decided to branch off and make her own dish, the Lentil Lada, an organic adaptation of the cheese enchilada, complete with lentils and fresh salsa.

Shari first became acquainted with the Dead in 1982 when she went to a Jerry Band show. She says that going to shows is an "addicting lifestyle," and that she still gets excited before every tour. "I jones for the shows," she says. "I come here and I get my fix, and then I go do my life, which is what happens between shows. And then shows are what alter that reality.

"I like the Grateful Dead because, for many people, they are the transportation to escape the decline of Western civilization," she explains. "It sorta takes us back to tribal economics and basic structures of the market place. It's about the closest to the Third World as we can get in the United States. I definitely grew up fantasizing about Third World countries, the cultures, the traditions and being creatures of habit. This whole thing, and especially the vending scene is a very cultural thing."

"I've always said there's a whole political coalition among vendors here," she says. "Sort of an unspoken thing. There's a routine and sort of a political way of dealing with getting into the lot. Parking lot politics. It's always the same people who are there hours before the lots open. All the major food vendors get together and sort of come up with common denominators of where everybody is going to be feeding into the show, where they're going to hang out, where the security headquarters are, where the extra parking lots are and to decide where the Shakedown is going to be."

Although she has done her share of touring in the past, Shari plans on slowing down a little. She still plans to go on tour, especially to West Coast shows, but not as extensively as she used to.

"Basically I've been doing this since I was seventeen, and I'm twenty-four now," she says. "In the last four years I've put a lot of miles on, and right now, I'm into staying home. I'm really ready to slow down."

The Lentil Lada
(serves 4–6 or 1 casserole dish full)

"I really like lots of herbs and spices, so it's kinda crazy because I put so much stuff in there," Shari says of her Lentil Lada. Right now, she is experimenting with different kinds of multicultural vegetarian foods.

1 lb. black beans (spiced with cumin and chili powder to taste)
1 lb. lentils
2 cups raw brown rice
2 cups quinoa (Shari explains that this grain only grows at a 6,000 feet elevation in the mountains of Peru. It is Peruvian for "the mother grain." "It is the only grain in the world that's a complete protein," she says. You can completely survive on it.") Quinoa can be found in health food stores and co-ops.
Brown in a skillet, add 2 cups water, and simmer.
1 or 2 cups steamed vegetables—try carrots, broccoli, zucchini
Salsa, to taste
organic whole wheat tortillas
Enchilada Sauce

Shari starts with a quick, brisk fry in olive oil, 3 tbs. garlic, 1 tsp. oregano, hot peppers to taste, 1 tsp. basil, 1 tsp. ginger, 3 tbsp. chili, 2 tbsp. cumin, soy sauce. Add 1–2 diced tomatoes and blend well. Keep on the side to pour over the enchiladas. Cook the brown rice and the quinoa. When finished cooking, add the black beans, cooked lentils, and steamed vegetables in a pot. Let simmer. Lay mixture in the middle of a tortilla. Do this with four to five of them, or enough to line a casserole dish. Top with enchilada sauce and tofu or rennet-free cheese. Bake at 350 degrees for 15–20 minutes. Serve with nacho chips and organic salad on the side.

Stylin' Fat Veggie Pizza

(makes 2 fat slices)

1 loaf fresh-baked whole-wheat French bread, sliced in half
mozzarella cheese, shredded
Tomato sauce (This, Elijah says, is the key. Don't use
    canned pizza sauce. Take time and make your own.)
Fresh-diced tomatoes or 1 28-oz. can stewed tomatoes
1 12-oz. can tomato paste
Fresh garlic, minced
Fresh oregano, to taste
Fresh basil, to taste
Lots of other spices you like to use!
Diced veggies (Try tomatoes, broccoli, red and green
    peppers. Olives or pineapple optional.)

Elijah suggests cooking the sauce for at least one hour
before it goes on the pizza. Add fresh garlic, basil, oregano,
and any other spice you want. Reuse any extra sauce on
more pizza, or in something else.
Slice the French bread in half. Spread the sauce on the
bread and sprinkle the grated mozzarella cheese on top.
Add the veggies. Top with diced tomatoes, broccoli, and
green and red peppers, all of which will make it colorful.
Elijah also suggests that you try adding pineapples and
olives.
Bake at 350 for about 20 minutes (depending on the oven
or how cooked you want it.)

Going on tour with friends is a time of closeness, a time when traveling partners feel like family, a traveling team. The atmosphere encourages many people to keep on touring. This cohesiveness is especially found among many of the food vendors who live in the San Francisco area, because there are so many of them. They are a vending family of sorts, staying in the same hotels and campgrounds together, helping each other out on the lot, and getting together for potluck dinners and birthdays.

As Elijah Tyler got to know other food vendors selling his Stylin' Fat Veggie Pizza, he quickly became friends with them.

"It's really nice because now a lot of us hang out as a group of friends outside of the shows, where we used to just hang out together for a few minutes here and there in between lots of busy work," he explains. "Now we're actually friends away from the lot, which is great. We've gotten to know each other, and we really rely on each other as friends. We can count on each other.

"For my birthday, we had a seventy-five-person potluck dinner and all the vendors cooked! It started to drizzle, so we threw up our tarps and we used all our ovens to cook and we used all our big tables to spread out a big buffet line. It was pretty intense."

For a few years, Elijah has made and sold the pizzas along many of the tours. He does it because cooking is one of his favorite activities.

"Ever since I started selling food, I wondered what other good stuff you could actually sell on tour," he says. "It's always been very important for me to figure good stuff to sell. And I started out with pasta. I thought it was tough to make a product that was really that special with something like pasta and still sell that much of it. Then the pizzas came along and they went over really well in the lot. People were way psyched for veggie pizzas. I don't think any-one was doing those when I started."

Elijah believes that he is so successful because of the fresh vegetables he puts on the pizza. Elijah says that broccoli is the key. "People all over the country, even at Giants Stadium (where they would much rather have pepperoni) like broccoli on [their pizza]," he explains.

One of Elijah's favorite things about going to Dead shows is traveling to new places. "I love being on the road," he maintains. "I've been traveling as often as I can around the country. I've gone a good ten to twelve round trips at this point. I just love the driving. I love the highways, I love camping out, I love the national parks in this country. I love a lot of the National Monuments, I love just checking things out. I basi-cally try to do a tour so that I've got the time when I'm not on tour to do those things freely, to not have to worry about a job when I decide to go to the Southwest for two weeks and just hang out at Bryce and Zion."

As long as the Dead keep playing music, Dave and his friend, Grizz, plan on touring with them, traveling around the country, seeing shows, and supporting themselves by making pizza. In between tours they'll try to find temporary jobs, otherwise, they say they'll keep going "until Jerry stops."

To get enough money to stay on tour, they made their original Fatty Fear Personal Pizzas, featuring a freshly made crust. It is a recipe Dave developed working at various restaurants while going to culinary school. In the lot, Dave usually cooks the pizzas, while Grizz sells the piping hot pies as they emerge from the oven.

"He loves to cook, but I won't let him do it sometimes," says Dave pointing toward Grizz who stands behind their fold-out table, serving. "But if I'm not in the mood, I go up there and do what he does, entertain, front of the house, you might say. People get interested, you know? They're like, 'What are you doing?' And you get to talk to people. I love that so much.

"This is our third show trying the pizzas," he continues. "We went from a fourteen-inch pizza to an eight-inch pie where it's easier and more economical for everybody. It's quick, fast, and instead of just grabbing slices off a pan, we give one whole pie. We just do it to go to the next show. We want to keep touring."

Like other Deadheads on tour, Dave and Grizz vend to support themselves, because they have no other job. They depend on the money they make to buy gas, tickets, food, and other traveling essentials. Without vending, they most likely would be stuck in the last city they were in.

"I love them," exclaims Dave of the band. "I heard bootlegs, and I said, 'I gotta see one of these shows.' I wanted to see the show, I wanted to hear the music they play so well. They're the cleanest cut band, ever. Ever. Nobody can do 'em. And I was an old Who fan. I've come to respect the band more just being there. They've gone through a lot of shit for the last ten years to be up there playing. I just love to hear them, man."

"I think we're going to run out of gas," he suddenly announces as their generator which runs the pizza oven kicks off and its loud whir is silenced to reveal the sound of a drum circle a few cars over. "Damn generator," he laughs.

"I think people keep coming back because you get a good feeling," explains Grizz. "People are so nice. You get your locals that are rowdy, but there's more kind people than that. I come back because I like the people. I love the atmosphere. I like to see babies and kids at these shows, because it's just going to keep going. It will keep the generations moving so people will still hear the music and love it. Love it as much as I do. I love them for what I'm able to do, so I can get to another show. The boys make me happy, that's for sure."

Fatty Fear Fresh Personal Pizzas
(makes 2 pizzas)

DOUGH

2 cups water, tepid between 100–115 degrees. (If it's warmer, the yeast could die.)

3/4 oz. active yeast

2 tbs. sugar

1 tsp. salt

5 cups white or wheat flour (add more if needed to make a firm dough)

SAUCE

1 28-oz. can pureed tomatoes

1 12-oz can Tomato paste

Oregano, salt, and pepper, season to taste, but use lots!

At least 6 cloves fresh garlic, minced to your taste. ("To me, a pizza should have lots of garlic," says Dave.)

Olive Oil

Mozzarella cheese, shredded—as much as you like

Veggies, to your taste. Try zucchini and onions! Sauté them first and add to the sauce or just sprinkle over the pizza before it goes in the oven.

Begin the sauce by sautéing the garlic in oil. Add the pureed tomatoes and tomato paste. Mix well and season with oregano, salt and pepper to taste. Let simmer for 1–2 hours.

To get the proper dough consistency, use 4 cups of flour to start, and continue adding as needed. Depending on what water and yeast you use, the amount of flour will need to be adjusted. "Sometimes it's funny," says Dave. "Yeast is pretty interesting. It feeds and it lives." Combine the remaining ingredients to make the dough.

Roll the dough with a rolling pin or press flat by hand. A rolling pin will make a round pizza crust. Dave says that the consistency of the dough should be much tighter than bread dough, but lighter than puffed pastry dough.

Once the dough is ready, spread on the sauce, mozzarella cheese, and more spices. Bake at 450 degrees for 20 minutes.

Harvest Earth Heart sits on a Mexican blanket, looking out into the parking lot at RFK Stadium, her arms covered in carob and honey. She has been molding Energy Nuggets under Bhakta's canvas umbrella. It's starting to rain on the Shakedown at RFK, and people are running to stand under the highway bridge which has become home to a group of Deadheads who are pounding away on drums in a large drum circle. The sounds echo through the crowd, and reverberate off the concrete supports which hold the highway, high above the Potomac River.

"It's so interesting the way all of us come together through the music of the Grateful Dead," says Harvest pensively. "It's a connection. All of everything that God did, was to make the Grateful Dead and come on through with the music. All from God. So is this," she says, holding up one of Nuggets chef Bhakta's Energy Nuggets. "This is all God. I'm not even rolling these goo balls. It's just the Lord."

By the middle of the East Coast summer tour, Harvest had begun traveling with Bhakta because he had extra space in his truck. Harvest and Bhakta are both committed to spreading the word of the Lord. For them, listening to the Grateful Dead is a good way to connect with the God within and outside themselves.

"My first faith in God came from just being here," she explains, referring to the parking lot and the people around her. "Learning everything about myself, being on the road is good. Because people are straight up, and you learn, and it's good, positive that way. Grateful Dead. I love the Grateful Dead, Lord.

"I live on the lot of the Grateful Dead," she continues. "They (venue security) say, 'Go home! Go home!' I say, 'I am home!'" she laughs. "All I want is to be able to go to the bathroom in a clean place."

Harvest has been going to shows since 1985 when she was in high school. "It was overwhelming in the beginning," she explains. "I was just taken aback by the Grateful Dead. But definitely somewhere, something different happened." she says, with a smile. "And then slowly, you see different things happening on the lot. You see a lot of people looking for God, in desperate ways and funny ways, and all sorts of things, and you see it. It's so interesting the way God shows us different things and different kinds of people."

One of the dishes that Harvest likes to vend in the lot is the Vegan Organic No Electricity Sprouted Wheat Berry Pizza. She sold them at the Phoenix shows in 1993 and found that people were ecstatic about the taste and the shape of the pizzas.

"When they came out, they were just so beautiful. They look so beautiful when they're wrapped in the circles. And then you can say something beautiful when you're talking about them, about Jesus. And then they'll ask you a question, and there we go!" she exclaims. "Spreading the word of the Lord around! That's good.

"It was so cool selling them," she explains. "The second night I was standing there, a woman came up to me. She loved them, and she had been telling these two sisters about these Wheel-of-Creation-Spiral-No-Electricity-Vegan Pizzas while inside the show. They had no idea that when they came out, I was going to be standing there. And they all just bought them. It was great. It was so high to sell them like that.

"It's really good to sell high food that is vegan because I think it's about purifying your thoughts and your physical body to go through the gates of Heaven," she adds. "So we want to unclog our body, as well as our thoughts, of mucous, animals and toxins. So then we are what we eat. So whatever is coming off our tongue, we can be more aware of. You know, spread the word!

"Eventually I'd like to have a little place where people can come to heal. You know, like maybe a campground or something like that, and I could do a whole sprout garden, an herbal garden, all the veggies, then maybe have a greenhouse, an avocado tree, and lemons and stuff. I'd like a big huge fat oven to bake the bread in, with all big huge fatty crystals sticking out of it. High Holy Bread. And just let people come there.

"We could have sewing and pottery, and I've always wanted to do stained glass. I'm good with my hands, creating things. A place that's respectful. Where people respect each other. And I've had these visions of spinning black wool, so probably a lot of sheep," she adds. "Everyone would be welcome. A church without walls. I'd like to have older people there, they have so much. And maybe lost animals. See, I'm so Virgo. I like to help people. I have six planets in Virgo, and my rising is Aquarius.

"Hello! Good morning, sister, hello!" She stops to greet a friend walking up to the blanket. "I'm not here to make money," she explains. "I'm not here for any other reason, and I used to think a lot more people were enlightened about the music. I hope a lot more people will be. That's what it's about. It's a good prayer. It's a prayer to go in and meditate on the Lord, and it's open for everyone. Open up your eyes, little darlin'!" She laughs.

Wheel-of-Creation-Vegan-Organic-No-Electricity-Sprouted-Wheat-Berry Pizza

(makes 2 spirals)

"It's unleavened bread, Bible bread," says Harvest. "It doesn't have yeast or anything in it. It's like Essene bread, with all the sprouted grains and stuff. It's interesting, you should try it!"

2 cups wheat berries
1 avocado, sliced
5 or 6 medium cloves garlic, minced
2 tomatoes, sliced
other assorted veggies!
Most co-ops and health food stores carry

wheat berries. Put them in water and sprout for 2 days. Keep rinsing them off. Put the sprouted berries through a wheat-grass grinder. It will come out in long strips. Wrap the strips into a spiral of life circle.

Needed: *A wheat-grass grinder*

Once in a spiral pizza shape, place it into the sun for half an hour. Or make them on a wood stove. It doesn't need to be that hot, just keep an eye on it. It will come out crusty on the outside and moist on the inside. "The crusty layer on the outside will seal the wonderfulness inside," says Bhakta of Harvest's pizza.

Mash the garlic in a garlic press and put on top of the spirals with sliced avocados and tomatoes. Harvest says anything can go on the top. Try spinach or broccoli.

"Everything I do, I offer up to God," says Harvest. "I'm just saying a prayer, while I'm baking."

✳ ✳ ✳

Paul and Marie and their dogs, Copernicus and Dante, share the same lifestyle. Along with their owners, the dogs go on tour, hang out, and even made an appearance at Paul and Marie's wedding. But they are most alike in that they, like their owners, are vegetarians.

Dante, three, and Copernicus, four, have been vegetarians for three years. Every two or three days Paul and Marie will make a huge batch of dog food from a variety of different ingredients that they come across. "Dogs, just like people, shouldn't eat the same thing all the time or you're not going to get what your body needs," asserts Paul.

The two have chosen not to feed their dogs meat for moral and ecological reasons. They've also read up on the subject and found that dogs can be healthy vegetarians. "We're not going to buy meat in dog food because murder is murder, no matter if you're eating it, or if it's your dog eating it," says Marie.

"If we're giving it to our dogs, it's still helping the process that is ruining the planet with pesticides, fertilizers, steroids, antibiotics," says Paul. "It's causing a problem, but most people don't see that. Ten years ago, I was like, 'Where's my hamburger?' I needed my hamburger. Since going to a vegetarian diet I see a lot more of the planet. Diet has to do a lot with consciousness. If you eat garbage, you are garbage."

Paul and Marie say the only problem they have making the veggie dog food is that it is difficult to prepare the potato-rice and bran dish on the road and away from a kitchen because of the quantity of ingredients that need to be mixed.

For years, Paul and Marie have gone on every seasonal tour, selling something or another out of their Earth-Kind Organic food selection. Now Marie says that they just go on summer tour to get their Dead "fix."

For Marie, going on tour these days is a mixed blessing. She thinks the Dead parking-lot scene has changed in recent years and it bothers her. "Recently there seems to be a lot of

Earth-Kind Miso Soup
(serves 4–6)

"This is not a specific miso recipe," says Paul. "You can do miso soup in 1,000 different ways. You kinda have to be a food mechanic. You have to use your knowledge of food and what goes together. There are different types of miso colors, kinds, and seasonal recipes. Some people drink miso tea.
"With miso soup, flavor is important, but so is color, flavor, textures," he continues. "You eat with your eyes before you eat with your mouth. If it looks bad, chances are it's not going to taste as good."

1 or 2 onions, sliced thin	2 cups vegetables, sliced,
Tamari—to taste, but use	any kind
lots	5 cups water
1/2 lb. mushrooms, sliced	Miso—to taste, but try
3–5 carrots, sliced	4 to 6 tablespoons

Caramelize the onions in tamari rather than oil to keep the fat content down. The sugars will come out and bring the desired sweetness.
After the onions are really soft, add water and then throw in the miso and vegetables, adding the hard ones first. Bring to a boil until they turn a bright color. Add more water if desired. Paul points out that it is important to time the vegetables correctly, don't overcook them.

Earth-Kind Dog Food

Paul and Marie created this recipe based upon a natural health recipe they found for dogs and cats. They make it by eye and compose the ingredients by what they find in their fridge. See if your dog likes it!

2 parts potatoes
2 parts oats
2 parts brown rice
1/2 part dried kelp
1/8 part nutritional yeast
A sprinkle of calcium powder
1 part tofu

1 part buckwheat and/or corn flour
1/2 part wheat bran
1/2 part fresh garlic
1/2 part sprouts and/or other assorted veggies
1/2 part assorted nuts

Dice the potatoes, then bake or boil them. Cook the oats and put them into a large bowl. Add dried kelp, the potatoes, nutritional yeast, calcium powder (provides basic vitamins and minerals); mix with brown rice. Periodically add buckwheat and corn flour to absorb some of the moisture and to include something different in their diet. Add wheat bran to the mixture.

Add fresh garlic to keep the fleas and bugs away. Depending on what is in season and inexpensive, add vegetables. "We give them greens," says Pat. "Sprouts are really good for dogs and for people." Chop the veggies up very fine, and then steam them. (They don't steam the sprouts). Put the vegetables through a food processor. Add tofu and nuts, which will provide protein. Blend in a processor or by hand. Mix everything together well. Blend again in a food processor if desired.

people spare changing. I can't afford to feed people because they spent their money on KB (Kind Buds) and alcohol. People can get two pieces of twine and sell it, instead of having to beg. But there is still so much good, and so much love in the music, and of course I'd much rather do this and spend my summers with Paul than have to be at a job somewhere.

"I used to get miracles all the time," she explains. "I never tried to bum everything else. You get a miracle when you deserve it, and when it's your karma, because you're a good person. You don't get a miracle because you have to beg for everything. You have to beg for your food, you have to beg for your ticket. You shouldn't be here if you can't take care of yourself."

"I'd walk around with my finger up [looking for a ticket], sometimes having money and people would say, 'Ticket's on me,' or, 'Here you go, sister.' I think that's a miracle, not walking around begging for everything."

Sweet Stuff

✳ ✳ ✳

During the winter of 1993, Melanie, Tara, Kelly, and Baye all left their homes, friends, and jobs to live and work in a ski resort town in Winter Park, Colorado.

Traveling from Milwaukee, Denver, and Cleveland, the four began living together and working as housecleaners and "T-shirt sales reps" or "T-shirt ladies." To take a break from their new jobs, they decided to go on tour a few months later to "get away from our normal lives and enjoy some concerts." The four toured in

Tara's small '85 Honda Civic hatchback which they say wasn't too bad; they were already used to cramped traveling.

To support their trip on tour, they sold Navajo Fried Bread, a dessert pastry, and Navajo Tacos, both recipes borrowed from Melanie's family who are Navajo Indians. The four took turns preparing the dough, frying it, and walking around with a tray, working as "the sales rep."

"My aunt gave us the recipe, so we're all practicing how to do it," explains Melanie. "The recipe has been in the whole tribe for a long time. Navajo Tacos and Fried Bread are really good."

At the Chinese New Year shows in Oakland, they just made the Fried Bread, but at the shows in Phoenix a week later, they began making the Tacos.

"The Tacos are with chili, onions, salsa, tomatoes, cheese, and lettuce. They're really good on top of fried rice," says Melanie.

The four say they go on tour because they love the band and the people they meet. Tara is especially attracted to the energetic feeling she gets inside the shows. "When I'm inside a show I have this great energy flowing through," she says. "Last night I got a miracle ticket and I was just so excited. I was talking to everyone and it was just like, *energy!*"

Navajo Fried Bread

(makes about 1–2 dozen, depending upon size)

4 cups flour (They suggest using very soft flour.)	2 tsp. baking soda
	Salt to taste
1 cup water	1/4 cup vegetable or canola
1 cup milk	oil

Mix ingredients together. Let rise for half an hour. Shape the dough into small round balls. Roll each out with a rolling pin, spreading on flour when too sticky to roll. When placed in the oil, each piece should be very flat and thin. Be willing to make mistakes. This is hard to do and it takes some practice. Deep fry in oil at about 375 degrees for about 10 seconds on each side, though it may take longer depending on how hot the oil is.

Pour honey and sprinkle powdered sugar on top.

Go to a show. Any show. You'll most likely see Bhakta, sitting under his big, white, canvas umbrella. His hands and arms are usually flecked with carob chips, peanut butter, coconut, and then moistened by honey as he rolls Energy Nuggets into small brown balls. Occasionally, a passerby will ask what he is making, and he will dare them to try the delicious Nugget by offering a deal. "Try it, if you don't like it, it's free," he'll announce. Inevitably, the person pays, happy to be eating the sweet, gooey ball.

Bhakta is one of many people on tour who believe that the Dead's music connects with their own spirituality, and the show is a spiritual experience in and of itself. A show is a meditation, a time to give thanks for the joy that the music has brought them, a time to get in touch with inner spirituality, and a time to dance with this spirituality.

"It shows me the path that's already inside myself that I can follow to find God," explains Bhakta. "Jerry just helps me find it. Right now I'm finding it inside, sometimes I find it outside, but usually you have to look inside to be able to listen to the music enough.

"Inside the show, you don't have to think or feel, or think about what you feel or feel what you're thinking. You're just there and one second is what the one second is, and the next second is the next second. It's like a progression, you have to be able to let go of the last note that was so beautiful in order to embrace the next note. So, it's not any feeling, but the lack of feeling makes you kind of satisfied in a way, because you don't have anything, and you don't miss anything.

"Everything from the tour, from the dance, is definitely my life," asserts Bhakta. "I like to think that everything is a reflection. The same way the material world is a reflection of the spiritual world, then tour is a reflection of non-tour. It's always a dirty mirror that we're looking through, so we can't really tell, but if we look hard enough, we can see the similarities and make our learning experiences expand in that way."

The "dance" he refers to is revered by many Deadheads, and it is a familiar sight in the hallways of a Dead show. Deadheads spin and move their bodies in bright colored, loose, flowy skirts that billow with each rotation. Watching groups of these dancers spinning and twirling can take your breath away. Their bodies flow along with the music, each person engaged in a choreographed dance of their own.

The act of spinning was practiced by the "Whirling Dervishes," of the Mevlevi Sufi order 1500 years ago. Sufism is an Islamic mystical discipline which envisions itself beyond religion, seeking preeminent unity of all faiths. Today, many still spin in praise of God or Allah, looking for physical and spiritual ecstasy through music and dance. It is believed that if one is truly focused and centered, dizziness is avoidable, for in your mind's eye you'll discover your true being, as the exterior world melts away. For those spinning, every thing around them is illuminated, and the spinners are better able to focus within themselves. For both Deadheads and some religions, spinning is said to bring the dancer closer to their spirituality, to a higher being, to God.

"When you're dancing, it's called breaking through," Bhakta says. "When you can't dance anymore and Jerry is just getting going, then you have to keep dancing. Once you really get into the flow, it's the whole instant karma thing, where you stub your toe and you know why. Or you get a ticket, or you don't get a ticket, or you dance, or you don't dance. Anything can be a lesson once you clean the dirt off the mirror. Then you can see all the reflections clearly. Then everything is a learning experience and everything is true perception.

"I feel like the Dead definitely make you see more," he continues. "The dance makes you aware on a different level, also, but that doesn't necessarily mean that you're going to like what you're aware of, or that you're going to be able to do anything about it when you wake up in the morning. I think it's all about perception, because it's already there. We're already feeling it."

Bhakta's name comes from the time he lived in a Krishna temple. The word "Bhakta" is Sanskrit for "devotee," or one who is devoted. He still keeps the name for it reminds him of what he wants to do in his life, which is, serve others.

"When you're in a Krishna temple, and you're first starting out, you're a student," he explains. "They call you Bhakta Dave, or Bhakta Jim, etc., and it means devotee, it means student, it means one who is devoted. It's kinda hard to translate. When I left the temple to come on tour (which is the first time I came on tour), I was all shaved up and everybody remembered that I was a Bhakta, but no one remembered my name, so they just started calling me

Bhakta. So it's good for me, because I could leave my old name behind and start a new life, but still always remembering that I'm just a student, that I'm just a Bhakta. And I've really taken to the part, because Bhakta, a devotee, is one who serves with devotion and my whole path is serving people, doing what people want me to do. Like Jesus said, all things to all men. You just have to be there to serve your brother, you know? Take the trash out or chop the firewood, or kick down ten dollars for the electricity, who knows? Spiritual counseling, recipe in a recipe book, there are so many ways for you to have a relationship with the Lord, to fill that gap of separation, because the Lord is inside of each of us, and if I serve you, then I'm having a relationship with the Lord.

Energy Nuggets

"This was the original Ganja Goo Ball recipe, except you don't put any of the ganja butter in it," says Bhakta. *"The ganja goo ball is usually gooey, and people are just so psyched to slurp down the ganja butter, that they're not really caring about the aesthetic appeal of it, but when you make Energy Nuggets, or non-Ganja Goo balls, there has to be more to it then just slurpin' down ganja butter. So people make them and try to add all this fancy stuff to try to make it right, but they don't really have the experience of making ganja goo balls or being around them. Anybody can mix peanut butter and honey together in a bowl, but it's one thing to be able to roll it up and keep it in the fridge for the week without it either melting or crumbling.*
"It has to do with making it. You can go make it all day long and have enough to feed everybody. Everybody does their little thing, this is my thing. Make it at home. More power to you."

4 parts peanut butter
3 parts honey
2 parts carob
2 parts raisins (if you like it raisiny)
1 part coconut (or more depending on how fine it is)

ADDITIONAL INGREDIENTS
Try adding pumpkin seeds, sunflower seeds, pistachio nuts, Rice Crispies, or crunchy millet,

→

Cinnamon too!
Add dried tropical fruits like papaya, dried persimmons and star fruit.
"Go to town with it," says Bhakta.

SUBSTITUTIONS
Peanut Butter—organic sesame tahini
Carob—ginger and ginseng replaces powdered carob, or use a little quinoa.
   "Sometimes we use ginseng powder, but it's hard to find organic ginseng," he says.
   "Then it comes out blonde, which changes the flavor."
Honey—try using molasses, maple syrup, brown rice syrup or barley malt. Keep it vegan.

TO MAKE THE ENERGY NUGGETS:
"You just have to feel it out," says Bhakta. "Put the carob in the container first, so it doesn't stick to the edges, you miss that, you blow it. Add carob all along the way, a little at a time." Add the remaining ingredients and mix together. Bhakta suggests that before you get too carried away with the carob, add some coconut. This will soak up some of the moisture from the honey. "Make a few batches before you get all crazy. Get the feel of it," he says.
Rolling the balls are a little more difficult. "You gotta have a feel for it," he says. "I don't know how to explain it, it's just a feel. You have to be able to put a little energy into it. A goo ball isn't an easy thing to roll. You have to knead it like dough. If you are a beginner, mix it in a bucket and get it to the point where you can stick it on a table and really work it. Sometimes it's better if you let it sit and let the coconut soak up some oil. Just work it, that's the whole thing."

"Everything is an offer to some god," says Bhakta. "You have to offer it, it's not just giving thanks that it was given to you. The Lord is giving us all these things. So when you're making these Energy Nuggets, you're not making them for you, you're not making them to sell on the lot, you're certainly not making them for any money or profit, you're making it for your brothers and sisters and you're working your energy into it. And you're putting your love into it, and you're offering it to the Lord within all of us out here. And you think about that when you're mixing it in the back of the truck, in the hotel room, when you're shopping in the Co-op, when you're counting your food stamps, and your whole life is like that. Whatever it is, you try to perceive it in such a way, that it is for the Lord. You don't have to change what you're doing. Offer it up. You can only do it because the Lord gave you the money, the emotional capacity, and the body. Give it back, because it just keeps reciprocating."

When he last timed himself, Paul Goeltz, chef extraordinaire and maker of the famous Oatmeal Chocolate Chip Raisin Banana Cookie, could make 150 cookies every seventeen minutes.

Now he has it down to a science: Paul spends hours before each tour mixing batter and pumping his three ovens full with trays of cookies. All so he can quickly pack them up and take them to shows.

"I still hate the baking," he laughs, for he has been making the cookies for some time. "Sometimes I'm at home and like, 'Fuck, I don't want to do that,' but I know that there'd be lots of people who'd be upset if they didn't find me."

Paul, who estimates he's seen about 300 Dead shows in his lifetime, has been making his celebrated cookie since 1989 when he and a friend were looking for something to sell in the lot instead of beer. Although now cooking solo, he has built considerable name recognition for his cookie enterprise because of their distinctive taste and his "big mouth."

"I really enjoy selling the cookies, the interaction with the people," he proclaims. "I know that there's a lot of people who really like the cookie and you feed off of that, and they feed off of that. I think a lot of people feed on me sometimes, because I'm out there just yelling and screaming. There have been times when I'm out there, and I'm not even yelling anything, and people know, 'That's him, that's Paul, that's where you get the cookies.' It's fun. It's a real high. I'm really into what I do."

Many of the long-time food vendors have created signs to advertise their food, but few are as colorful as Paul's. When his cookies began to take off, Paul realized that he needed a logo, some recognizable symbol, so a friend created a clown sign for him. Since then a yellow, purple, and black clown wearing a jester's hat has become his trademark.

"People have to recognize you," he explains. "At the time I was going through a period of beards, long hair, short hair, and different stages of freakiness. People were never real sure if it was me, except for my voice, so I felt the need to have something so people could associate that sign with where you could find the goods. A lot more people know what spot I'm in and they head right there. Often the first thing you see is that stupid clown sign," he laughs.

The Oatmeal Chocolate Chip Raisin Banana Cookie
(makes 20 cookies)

3 cups oatmeal
1 1/2 cups chocolate chips
1 1/2 cups raisins
1 1/2 cups banana
1 1/2 cups flour
2 1/2 sticks butter
1 egg
1/2 cup honey
3/4 cup brown sugar
Salt to taste
1 tsp. baking soda
1 tsp. each: cloves, nutmeg, allspice, cinnamon
1 tsp. vanilla

Melt the butter and let cool. In a bowl, mix the vanilla, honey, spices, brown sugar, egg, and other soft stuff that mixes well. Will make a gooey mess.
When the butter has cooled down (so it won't cook the egg) pour into the bowl. Add the banana, raisins, chips, etc. Next add flour and oats and mix well. Roll into balls and cook at 350 degrees for 17 minutes. This should make about 20 big cookies.

Summer in the desert is pretty intense. It is a climate where the overwhelming heat overtakes everything: the horizon, the sky, and the mountains. From every corner the unrelenting heat expands and rises above the barren land. It is just this harshness that will alter just about any reality.

So when Las Vegas temperatures soar past 110 degrees, and the dusty winds kick up, you feel as if a hairdryer set on high is enveloping your body. It is on summer days like this that even the most daring gambler doesn't dare venture outside.

Picture this massive heat with 40,000 Deadheads hanging out in the parking lot of the Sam Boyd Silver Dome at the end of June 1994. Throw in little or no cloud cover and a temperature of 120 degrees. The result is a lot of dehydrated people who are dying for anything with water or ice.

When Brian Ebzery and Mike Schaefer decided to go to the '94 shows in Vegas, they knew that selling Shaka Shaved Ice would be successful.

The two, who call themselves "the Freeze Brothers," went to Vegas to take one last vacation before the summer rush in Tahoe City began. There, they run a shaved ice cart called Rainbow Refreshments. "We decided to come down here where it's a little warmer, because it's still cool up there (in Tahoe City). It's perfect for a place like this, 120 degrees, and ten fruity flavors to choose from," he laughs.

Brian, a fish bartender at a seafood bar, (he says the job is similar to a bartender, but he slings fish tacos instead of cocktails and beer) and Mike, a ski shop worker, started their shaved ice business last March. "It's fun," says Brian. "People like it in town, and up there we have blenders and we make fresh fruit smoothies and kinda go off a little."

At the shows they make sure to bring natural syrup for people who want shaved ice but not all the sugar. "People are down on having sugary things, so we make sure to get ones that have at least some natural flavors," he says. "Ours have a lot of natural sugar, but they also have natural flavors."

Brian has been going to Dead shows since 1984. He thinks that the best thing about seeing the Dead is listening to "Jerry's jams." "When he plays guitar really loud and hard, that's my favorite. Ear-splitting music of Jerry Garcia pretty much does it for me," he explains.

But he also loves going to shows for the tour food. "I'm a bit of a connoisseur on tour," he claims. "All the food that's going around, it's great. Big fat egg rolls take the prize. Those things are huge! And grilled cheese is always a good choice for an after concert stomach settler. Have to have that.

"I'm a bit of an ex-Deadhead, I must confess," he says. "The whole thing just kinda shut down for me two years ago. I was into it in a big way for a couple of years, since 1984, the first time I ever saw the Dead, until Chicago of '91. I was fairly addicted. A certain keyboard player kicked the bucket right after that and I think the band lost a lot of soul when that happened. I think a lot of Deadheads will admit that. That was kind of the crux in my Grateful Deading career. I finished up with some great shows, but I started getting too critical.

"The venues have changed. The venues I used to get into were just a kick in themselves. Just to go hang out in Berkeley and stumble over to the Greek Theater, or see them at Red Rocks, and camp out and just have a whole experience of camping. Now this is probably the best place for them. They need an indestructible city to play in because it just gets too trashed. The places they used to play where they would allow camping right in the parking lot, like Irvine and Frost, that was such a cool thing. The scene just kinda continued on and it was a lot less stressful. This is nice though, being down here in the hot sun and all coping together."

Shaka Shaved Ice
(serves 2)

"We're selling ice," says Brian. "Ice with syrup on it for a fair price, for some really hot people."

2 cups crushed ice or freshly fallen snow
1 cup squeezed, bottled or frozen fruit juices: orange, grapefruit, apple juice, etc.
Try adding the fresh-squeezed juice of other fruits to give it a kick: lemons, limes, kiwis, strawberries, etc.
Sugar—to taste
Water—use if a slushy—shaved ice is desired

Needed: An ice machine, freeze cup, crushed ice, or freshly fallen snow if it's winter.
"To make quality shaved ice, you need to use a machine, a freeze cup, crushed ice or freshly fallen snow," says Brian. "If you have a good blender, see if it will chop the ice very fine."

In a bowl, mix fresh squeezed fruit juice, fruit, sugar, and water. Pour this mixture over snow or blended ice. Eat in a cup and chill out!

It is the first night of the annual Chinese New Year Shows, and the horizon behind Feather Davis is heavy with clouds. Feeling a bit chilly outside the Oakland Coliseum, she stands with trash bags full of organic popcorn next to her feet. Equipped with shakers of cayenne, nutritional yeast, and garlic, she is selling small bags of popcorn for a buck. It is one of her favorite recipes, a snack she has eaten all her life.

"I've been eating it since I was a kid," she explains. "My uncle has been following the Dead since he was a kid. He lived in his bus, and he'd come park in front of our house and sometimes his girlfriend would come in and make us popcorn. I just started eating tons of it like that."

Karma Korn
(serves 2)

1/2 cup raw organic popcorn
Olive oil
Tamari, to taste
Nutritional yeast, to taste
Garlic powder, to taste
Cayenne to taste
Dill, to taste

Feather suggests adding as much olive oil as you would butter. This gets the popcorn wet, which allows the yeast, garlic powder, cayenne, or dill to really stick when sprinkled on top. For a salty taste, sprinkle on extra tamari. But be careful with the cayenne, it's hot!

Pop the popcorn (try popping it in a wok!), add the oil and mix around well. Sprinkle on more toppings to taste. Try them all!

To help pay for gas and tickets, Feather usually sells organic juice and popcorn. Like many Deadheads, she has concerns about eating pesticide-laden foods and is a proponent of organically grown foods. "Organic is just about all I'll do," she remarks. "I was raised on natural food, so it was pretty easy for me. My mother was into organic. She grew everything out of the garden, and made everything from scratch."

To Feather, the Grateful Dead's music is about understanding the energy and the connection that so often flows between the band and the audience at a show.

"I've been playing with the idea of bringing my sister to the show, because I really want to share with her how incredible it is. I'm thinking, well, maybe get her in a nice flowy skirt or something. Maybe she'll get it. But then I was thinking, I wonder if some of it is the familiarity with the music. I'm just so in love with Jerry's voice. It took me a few times to really hear that. As you get to know it, you get to really see what's going on."

For Feather, listening to the Dead is a good meditation, a way to practice tuning in with herself and the earth.

"For me, I get a real connection from the earth. Bringing the energy of the yin, the earth, up into the sky, into the yang, and bringing the yang down into the yin, I just feel like this circuit, this connection between earth and sky. When I'm dancing, I feel like I'm dancing on the energy, and I feel like I'm not even touching the ground, I'm floating. I haven't experienced that anywhere else. It really brings me there.

"Sometimes I'll get in there and feel disconnected. I'll just kinda bumble and trip around and I'll just get so disappointed, so I'll sit down and focus and watch, which is neat because I usually never watch. I find a place behind the stage where you can see right in there and check it out. Usually I'm just feeling it, and the notes are coming through me, and I feel like an expression of the notes.

"That's my highest state, that's where I'm totally in love, just being there, and flying. That's one of the most spiritual places that I've been able to find, because for me, meditation is just such a practice. I'm always practicing, I never feel like I've gotten there, but when I'm dancing, I've gotten there. That God state. That's where home is," she laughs. "And I'm always trying to get back."

Warren's camper is warm with the sugary smell of crepes cooking. He stands next to his stove flipping each crepe with care. It is only eleven o'clock in the morning, yet he already is cooking Strawberry Crepes, a dish which he will continue to make throughout the three day concert and camping weekend at Autzen Stadium in Eugene, Oregon.

"This is not just a concert, but a way of life," he says in a soft voice as he flips. "People can either be homeless or go on welfare lines or they can try to do something to make a living. This is one of the ways for the alternative community to have a respectable way of life."

For the shows, Warren wanted to make crepes, so he could use the strawberries that he grows to "let people experience Oregon strawberries, being organic and such."

Warren sometimes vends at Dead shows, but most of his vending days have been spent at the Annual Oregon Country Fair, a three-day festival, which some claim to have the same atmosphere of the original Woodstock. Warren himself likens the event to Woodstock. He was there three decades ago.

"When Woodstock occurred, it was a kind of birth of consciousness and evolution on what people thought, and people's minds were opened to new ideas," he declares. "It forced people to open up because of the natural linking that they had from the rain, from the starvation element of being cold, from all having to deal with everything on the same level. It unified people, where most concerts today are just a big

Strawberry Crepes
(makes 8–10 crepes)

1/3 cup of sugar
1 1/2 cups flour
3 eggs
1 to 1 1/3 cup of water
1/3 stick of butter or margarine
Fresh strawberries, sliced
Fresh bananas, sliced
Crushed Hazelnuts, toasted
Chocolate Sauce—Melt your own, or buy sauce

Needed: A stainless steel crepe pan

Mix the batter together. Pour a small amount into a stainless-steel crepe pan. Add sliced strawberries and bananas inside. Fold over and flip carefully until lightly brown on both sides. Sprinkle hazelnuts and chocolate sauce on top.

party. It was like for the first time being exposed to the sun, and just falling in love with it. That initial awakening is like a rebirth, and that is why Woodstock was unique.

"The dream, we thought at the time, would be here forever because once you're aware of something, how could you let something so precious slip away? Most people didn't respect it, so it's gone. Collectively, people need to realize that the collective potential they have as people can inevitably free them and give them the same power as corporate business bosses and international bankers."

Warren remembers working at the Bethel site, and cleaning up for weeks after the concert ended. "There were probably a couple thousand sleeping bags buried in the mud, and a couple hundred thousand pairs of shoes that were dug out," he explains. "The hog farmers fed whomever wanted to stay for those weeks, to help them clean up and get the place back together. They were trying to nourish a way of life and show people that food is the least you have to worry about when working together. It just kinda comes with the agenda.

"Here's another fruit crepe, anyone want another fruit crepe?" he asks his friend outside. "Strawberry, Banana Crepes!" his voice floats through the lot, becoming meshed with ten or fifteen other vendors' voices.

Like many vendors, Warren worries about the security at venues. His perception is that, like Woodstock, the community, the artisans, the magicians, the way of life at Dead shows needs to be encouraged, not policed.

"The way of life itself needs to be nourished," he states. "People who promote the concerts need to realize that they also need to respect why people follow the Dead, and deal with the reality, not the legalities of it. Most of the outdoor concerts have already been stifled throughout the country."

Warren believes that Dead shows are, "close to the idealism of wanting to gather and experience harmony and brotherhood and at the same time be able to sustain and make a little money. People come to experience the freedom that they never had in their life and walk away, some jealous, some envious, some content, but all knowing that they are probably missing something."

When Teri Jasman brought her baked goodies to the 1994 shows in Seattle she didn't want to worry about selling the desserts for gas and ticket money. Instead, she decided to make trades for her brownies and banana bread. "I decided this morning to take trades and see what the Universe would bring me," she laughs. "So far I got a stupid hat."

Baking brownies and bread is a ritual that Teri performs to get ready for Dead shows. Before she goes on tour, she "bakes her brew" at her home in Arcata, California.

"It's just a two- or three-day run of mass baking," she says. "It's good work to do before the show, because it totally focuses me and I think about what I want to get out of the scene and what I'm there for. And I bake and bake and bake and bake and pack it all up. It's a good little thing to do."

For part of the year, Teri lives in Arcata where she graduated from Humboldt State University. When in Arcata, she works as a healer with children that have developmental disabilities. The rest of the time, she is on the road, traveling to various areas along the West Coast. She says she loves that her clients respect that she is a free spirit and only in town part-time.

"I've lived for five years on the scene," she explains. "Within the last six months I've found my niche in Arcata with a good job. I always had to leave Arcata to make my money in the Dead scene to live there. Now I don't have that excuse anymore, so I'm just here to be here and when I'm there, I have a sole purpose."

Teri plans to write children's books, to aid them in getting through difficult periods in their lives. "I'm working on a book for kids who have been molested," she says. "A book for healing. I think the world is getting so harsh, that it's time that there are more kids' books that deal with what they're going through."

"I know what I'm doing is helping people," she adds. "I know exactly who I'm helping and what I'm doing, so I can feel good about making my money doing that. You give a lot of yourself, a lot of your loving energy. I'm pretty much paid to just be a loving light. A lot of these kids can't get it from their families."

Teri's Vegan Banana Bread
(makes 2 loaves)

This is a recipe which Teri has been making for years. It is all vegan. She uses the egg substitute in place of butter or dairy products.

5 or 6 overripe bananas
Egg substitute (1/3 cup flour, 1 1/3 cups water)
3 cups flour
1/2 cup sugar, maple syrup, honey, date sugar
1/2 tsp. baking soda
1/2 tsp. baking powder
1/3 cup oil (or 1/3 stick margarine)
1/2 tsp. vanilla
Salt—a pinch

In a thick saucepan, whisk 1/3 cup flour and 1 1/3 cup water over medium heat for 10 minutes. Let cool, then add 1/2 cup sugar (or honey, maple syrup or date sugar). Add 5 or 6 overripe bananas, vanilla, oil (or margarine), and mush up.
In a separate bowl, sift together 3 cups flour, baking soda, baking powder and a pinch of salt.
Sift together with the wet mix. The texture of the batter should be very elastic. Blend well and bake at 350° for 25–35 minutes.

At the 1993 shows in Richfield, Ohio, Theresa and Russ Morgan's Banana, Zucchini, and Carrot Bread slices rose to the top of the vending market and sold out within the first hour at one dollar a slice. Russ and Theresa had just begun baking bread at home when they decided to bring a bunch of the loaves to the shows. They gave away a substantial amount to spare-changing, hungry Deadheads, yet they still ended up making enough to pay for gas and a place to stay.

"We made bread for this tour because we wanted to sell things that weren't already in the market," said Russ. "There already are a lot of burrito-type fried foods, and people get really bored with that. Besides, everybody needs to eat nutritious food, but not everyone does. So many people will spend five dollars to get high on a balloon of nitrous, when they can spend five dollars here and have protein and vitamins."

"I thought the food went really well," continues Theresa. "At least it's something that somebody can use. I'd much rather sell something that people are going to have some use out of. And there'll be some good there. Not everybody thinks that way."

The two recently bought a 1961 International Harvester Metro Van, which according to them looks like an old milk truck. "You'll never see another one like it in your life. It's a classic," says Russ. "We wanted to get a stove with an oven, so that we can actually bake the bread in there. That's why we got the van, so we could make the breads and stuff, but we also wanted to have different things that we made and sell. A couple of drums or whatever, some baskets."

The couple plan on touring in the van, then later living in it when they move out West and need to save money. "We want to go and try to buy some land, we're not sure where, so we're going to drive out there and pick the place that we like the best," she says. "I don't want to go to California. Everybody goes there."

Besides cooking, Russ does leather and

woodwork and Theresa sews dresses while on tour. They both love being part of the scene, which Russ thinks is "a traveling society that can set up in a matter of minutes at any point on the road."

"I started going to shows about ten years ago," Theresa explains. "And there is no other place or event that could make me feel the same way as I do when I'm there. If I could find something else, maybe I'd consider that, but there isn't anything. It's very exciting, but very relaxing to me. Especially when you have to go to work every day, it's a great escape. Eventually, maybe we won't have to do that. Maybe we can live it. I think it's something I'll never give up."

Beautiful Breads
(makes 2 loaves—each with 12 slices)

3 cups grated or chopped zucchini, banana or carrot, your choice

3 eggs (They've heard you can substitute papaya for the egg to make it vegan.)

1 cup oil (peanut, safflower, or canola)

2 cups sugar

3 tsp. vanilla

3 cups whole wheat flour, sifted

1 tsp. baking soda

1/4 tsp. salt

2 tsp. cinnamon and nutmeg

1 cup nuts (optional)

Grease two loaf pans. Preheat the oven to 350 degrees. Grate or chop the zucchini, bananas or carrots. Set aside. Beat eggs and oil well, and add sugar and vanilla. Sift the flour, baking soda, salt, and cinnamon together. Add to the egg-and-oil mixture and beat well. The batter will be stiff. Fold in the zucchini, banana, or carrots and add nuts. Divide into pans and bake for 45 minutes to one hour, or until a toothpick is inserted in center and comes out clean.

Note: If making Banana Bread, use very ripe, almost rotten bananas. Follow the "browner the better" rule. Theresa and Russ also suggest soaking the bananas in very strong coffee. Puree the banana and soak it in the coffee while you're mixing the other ingredients. "It gives it a really good flavor," they say.

Note: For the non-sweet breads (zucchini and carrot), orange juice can be substituted for milk to make it sweeter and vegan.

Willem Jewett is another recent inductee to the Grateful Dead scene. But he was not as impressed as other newcomers. An avid bike racer who has spent time vending to the bike-racing crowd, Willem was taken aback by the scene at the Highgate, Vermont, show when he and his friend, Donald, were vending Apple Space Cakes.

"We've been bike racing for a while and we're pretty in tune with our bodies and we cook really healthy, organic food. It just really surprised us. Last night we camped over there," he says, pointing beside the dusty field that the Dead are about to play on. "I know it's all supposed to be peace and love, but, man, it seemed like a lot of negative energy. I was astounded by the amount of drugs. I mean, I'm not into the 'go-and-do-drugs' thing, but it's really excessive to me. I see these people stumbling around and they're sleeping with their faces in a pile of ashes from the fire. It's really kinda hard to handle. It just gives me really sad feelings for people. You know what I mean?" he asks. "I should've just gone in and listened instead of trying to do something else."

Willem has been bike racing for the last seven years and as a part of the hobby, helps his friend cook for the biking community. "We just go there and serve burritos. I like preparing natural food, going to events, and serving it. People really enjoy it, so we thought we'd come up here and do the same thing." So they made up a batch of Apple Space Cakes, a recipe derived from a racing friend.

"I just like sharing really good food with friends," he explains. "We have a lot of potluck suppers and stuff. We go bike riding and invite people over and cook a lot, too. It's a real important part of life, you know! The air you breathe and the food you put into your body, it's a lot of who you are."

After graduating from the Northwestern School of Law in Portland, Oregon, one month before the Highgate show, Willem is planning on slowing down his bike-racing tours and working as a lawyer.

"Biking has been part of my life, and it's kinda going to be difficult now being a lawyer, finding a different level of intensity," he says. "I'm very intense when I race. It's a physical challenge, you really put yourself on the line and kinda go beyond what you think you can do a lot of times. Also, you can get out into places you never imagined you'd be.

"When I was in law school, I commuted on my bike every day for three years. I didn't use a car. I think a bike is the most amazing machine made because of its efficiency and what it really could do for us. In other countries, people don't own cars, they own bikes to get around. It's going to be different these next few years when I'm working behind a desk and I can't get out there, get in front of the pack and ride with the big boys. Hopefully it'll be part of my life."

Apple Space Cakes
(a.k.a. Jenergy Bars)
(makes about a dozen cakes, depending on how large you shape them)

Willem's friend, Jen Mynter, creator of the Apple Space Cakes or Jenergy Bars, also bike races. She makes the Space Cakes as energy bars because they contain no eggs or oil.

WET INGREDIENTS
2 cups of rolled oats or rye flakes
1 can of apple juice concentrate (For variation, try organic red raspberry juice, or any other juice. They suggest a sugarless juice.)
1 glob of tahini, almond butter or peanut butter
1 really ripe banana, mashed
1/3 or a 5-oz. jar of brown rice syrup or honey

DRY (Add enough dry ingredients until the mixture reaches a cookie consistency. It will not be as wet as muffin batter.)
2 cups or so brown rice flour, whole wheat pastry flour, or corn meal (Jen suggests using spelt flakes, or corn flour, but any will do.)
A sprinkle of raisins, dates, or any other dried fruits
A sprinkle of walnuts, crushed
Cinnamon, to taste
1 tsp. baking powder
Salt

Soak the oat or rye flakes in 1 can of apple juice. This will act as a sweetener. Jen usually uses brown rice syrup, but for the shows, Willem used honey. Add either. Add a glob of almond or peanut butter, or tahini and the mashed banana. Let that sit for a few hours to absorb moisture, otherwise the oats and rye are dry and crunchy. Mix the dry ingredients and add to the wet ingredients. Mix together, and spread the mixture over a cookie sheet or shape into cookies on a baking tray. Jennifer sometimes sprinkles corn meal over it before she bakes.
Bake at 350 degrees for about 15–20 minutes or until brown. Let cool, then cut.

Pasta

✳ ✳ ✳

Rain is pouring down on Washington, D.C., and the surrounding areas that encompass the parking lots of RFK Stadium. All those walking around the Shakedown without an umbrella or a vehicle to sit in, run for cover under the highway overpass. Beneath the overpass sit various cars and buses, some of which have taken advantage of the rain-free vending under the covering. One of them is Rachel and Dupree's 1965, twenty-one-window rag-top Volkswagen. The two sit in the bus chopping vegetables and beading Rachel's jewelry. Carefully placed upon the edge of the VW's windows are an assortment of yo-yo's, for the two are avid yo-yo'ers. "It's a great sport," one of them proclaims.

As the sky darkens towards nightfall, the rain stops and the masses who gathered under the bridge begin to move on. Now there is room for Rachel and Dupree to assemble their rickety table, which they cover with a purple tapestry, candles, and a display plate of their Curried Vegetables on Peanut Sesame Ramen Noodles.

"When people find out it's Ramen noodles, they're always so shocked," remarks Rachel. "They're like, 'Oooh, Ramen Noodles! Oh, my God.' Those noodles are the total starving-student thing."

The two cut and prep their food the night before shows. They do all their cooking on a forty-dollar stove that they bought before summer tour.

"I like cooking on the road," Rachel says. "It makes me feel much more at home to have the stove in the bus. We have four burners, so we can cook the noodles at the same time as we cook the sauce. But dishes suck. It's hard dealing with dishes."

The 1994 show at RFK marked the second summer that Rachel and Dupree had been touring together. They met at the 1993 show in Buffalo when Rachel asked him for a ride to get to the next show in Louisville, Kentucky.

"I wanted to go to Louisville, so I bought a ticket beforehand, and I set out to find a ride," remembers Rachel. "I decided to go over to where all the school buses were parked, 'cause I figured I'd have a better chance of finding a ride. Dupree's bus was the first one I went up to. There was some girl sitting in the driver's seat, so I thought it was her bus, and I asked her if they had room for another rider and she said she didn't think so. I almost walked away, but then she said, 'Oh, you should ask the driver.' So I asked Dupree, and he said, 'Do you have gas money?' And I said, 'Yep.' And so I hopped in his bus and the rest is history."

After they finished out that tour, Rachel and Dupree moved to Santa Cruz, but now they're considering making the move to northern California. They may migrate towards the Yuba River area, the place where Dupree was raised and is named after. (His given name is Yuba, but for as long as he can remember he has gone by Dupree.) Wherever they go, Rachel plans on going back to school to be a sign language interpreter, and Dupree will continue working on Volkswagens.

"I've been going to school for the last three years, and I think I'd like to go through a training program to be certified as a sign language interpreter," says Rachel. "I've never had a major. Just general education classes. I've learned a lot on the road. In school, it's just mind food, it's reading and thinking a lot. But when you're on the road, it's interacting with people and understanding people, and connecting with people. It's more having to do with people than just in your mind."

Rachel and Dupree get on the road to see Dead shows for the same reason so many Deadheads do. They want the freedom, the timelessness, and the minute-to-minute living of life that they find on the road.

"It's fun to be an outlaw," Dupree says of touring. "This is one of the last great adventures left for us in the United States. If we weren't here, we'd probably be sitting home watching cable TV or something. It's fun to have a feeling of community, and extended family. It's just a good party."

Vegan Veggie Curry on Peanut Sesame Noodles
(serves 4–5)

Dupree invented this dish when he tried to come up with something else to make with Ramen noodles besides using "the yucky flavor packets." One day, he just added peanut butter and other spices, and "it turned out good."

VEGGIE MIXTURE

3 cups potatoes, diced
2 cups carrots, diced
1 cup onions, diced
1 cup celery, diced
2 tbs. margarine
5 tbs. curry
2 cloves garlic, crushed
1 cup broccoli, diced

1 cup peas
1 tsp. tamari
2 tsp. ginger, grated
3/4 cup apples, diced
1/4 cup raisins
1/2 cup apples
4–5 tsp. corn starch
1 1/2 cup water

PEANUT SESAME NOODLES

3 or 4 pkgs. Ramen noodles or thin Chinese
   noodles
1 cup peanut butter

3/4 cup hot sesame oil
2 tsp. tamari
Ginger—pinch

Steam the potatoes and carrots in any conventional steamer.

In a very large skillet, sauté the onion, celery, and garlic in margarine. Add curry to taste. Add the water, broccoli, peas, and the steamed potato and carrot mixture.

Add a splash of tamari, the ginger, apples, and raisins. Let simmer for 5–10 minutes.

At this point if the mixture is watery, add some of the cornstarch to thicken. Add more curry and garlic if desired.

Prepare the packages of Ramen noodles (discard the enclosed flavor packets) and drain when finished.

For the Peanut Sesame Noodle sauce, mix the peanut butter in 1/4 cup hot water to dissolve the peanut butter. Add 2 tsp. tamari, hot sesame oil, and a pinch of ginger

Serve the mixture over noodles and enjoy!

Matt Blau and Kristin Anderson love to cook and to share their culinary creations with others. So when the Dead came to the small northern town of Highgate, in Vermont, they were there to make fresh squeezed lemonade and fresh Cold Sesame Noodles.

"We like bringing people a taste of what we do and what we love," says Matt. "We might be able to make money from peanut butter and jelly sandwiches, but we just don't want to. It's not fun for us. We'd really wanted to do sushi, but we couldn't do it cheaply enough."

"We enjoy working with fine food," adds Kristin. "We don't want to just make and sell slop."

The two own a catering business called the Moveable Feast, a food service which specializes in vegetarian, vegan, and natural cuisine. Since 1992 they have provided natural

sandwiches, vegan sushi, and other vegetarian creations for three health food stores in the Brattleboro, Vermont, area.

"We're kinda just starting out," says Kristin. "This business is solid, and we're starting up with other stuff. Matt has traveled all over the world, and we really like international food. Multi-ethnic food. We also like to use natural food as much as possible, and introduce people to food that they wouldn't ordinarily eat."

"I love the fact that we can work for ourselves and I love working with food," explains Matt. "It's one of the basic things that I feel one can do in this life, it's sort of where it's at. It seems like you either work with food, heal the sick, or do one of those things that is sort of organic. I love having my hands in food. I like it much better than pushing pencils around paper or anything else that I've tried."

In the past, Matt has tried his hand as a real estate broker and owning a sushi bar, both in New York City. Now he and Kristin work in the business while Kristin finishes her studies in Ethnobotany. She has spent a considerable amount of time in Guatemala studying the influx of western medicine on the traditional medicinal systems of the Guatemalan Highlands.

"It was amazing," she remarks. "Just the people. Being around people who still have a sense of what is important. It's important to eat, it's important to love your family, it's important to work the ground. It was a really vital time. I love the country."

When not cooking, Matt and Kristin live without water or electricity in a rural house they recently built themselves. "Matt and I live on 200 acres of land," explains Kristin. "The person who owns the land said that I could build on it if I ever wanted, and I said, 'All right.' I had no idea what I was getting into. I did my blueprints on napkins, and then built the thing, and it's beautiful. It's post and beam. There are two parts. There's a twelve-by-twenty cabin. Then a twenty-by-twenty one-and-a-half story addition. I'm still building it. I was going to go solar, but it just is not solar conducive. A friend of mine is an electrical contractor, and we wired the house for hook up. I don't need power and I'm not going to do it anytime soon."

Cold Sesame Noodles
(Serves 5)

3 tbs. smooth organic peanut butter
3 tbs. warm water to thin
1 tb. toasted sesame oil
2 tbs. tahini
1 tsp. fresh ginger, ground. Grate or juice it!
1 tsp. fresh garlic, ground
2 tbs. rice wine vinegar
1 tb. sugar or honey
2 tbs. tamari
1 tsp. rice wine
1 pound of pasta (Use regular linguini, or a good Italian pasta.)
Cucumbers
Scallions

In a bowl, mix all of the ingredients (while the pasta is cooking). Once the pasta is done, add it to the bowl and mix to coat. Chill and marinate overnight in a little sesame oil and tamari.
Garnish with cucumbers and scallions.
"If you stumble across something for which there are no words, you can almost be sure it's meditation," says Matt.

It is the last night of the blustery warm hot in Las Vegas. Jeff Shelton and Amelia Josey are tired and really hot, as the night air is still in the nineties. As the parking lot begins to empty out and dust kicks up around them from the exiting tires, they clean out the bowls and utensils they used earlier in the night to make High Thai. They are both excited. It is the first show of the tour for them.

"When we were in Vegas, we realized we were going to be together and we were at the show, and I just felt really euphoric, because I was thinking I could do this all summer. We're going to do this styling," says Jeff. Amelia and Jeff have both been touring since the late eighties. It is one of their favorite activities they do together. While on tour, they made High Thai to pay for gas and tickets. They loved the vending, but found that going on tour is a lot different when you're making large amounts of food.

"Touring is stressful when you're doing food," says Amelia. "You don't get very much sleep and you have to really work together. I don't think you could do it with anyone you didn't love. I think that's definitely a requirement, the teamwork that's involved. You have to be able to just be in synch all the time. We really love having all the time on the road together in the car, just the two of us, driving across the country and then the time together at the shows and being able to reflect on it. It's like we're best friends, tour buddies, and romantic partners.

"Vending is great," she continues. "I'm really enthusiastic about vending, I love it. I like what we're providing, especially now with the hemp seeds, because hemp seeds are a whole food with all the essential amino acids. I'd like to promote that view and get it out there.

"I think it's really positive for your self-esteem when people want your food, and it's great providing them with healthy food. It's like a service, and it's lots of fun. You recognize your customers, they recognize you. Especially because people have been really enthusiastic about our food."

For Amelia, going to Dead shows has always been a way to grow and learn about herself.

"Growing up in South Carolina, it's very conservative," she explains. "The Dead was a way to travel around and be a free thinker. At first it was all the fun, the freedom, and the heartfelt love for the music itself. Then it progressed to an inner spiritual growing process. It had a lot to do with becoming a woman, kinda going through the bloom and blossom thing through the Dead. I think I've gone through a lot of peaks and valleys with the Dead. It's always a place to go to center."

"I like the freedom of everything, the music, the scene," adds Jeff. "It's definitely a circle with the scene and the music. I like the diversity and the freedom that's involved with the Dead, even though it seems to be getting less and less free."

Jeff and Amelia named their Thai recipe after the Dead tune, "High Time." "We were in Deer Creek the second night, we had our tickets, and we were breaking down the set-up right before going into the show," says Amelia. "And Jeff says, 'We should write, "Having a high Thai, living the good life." ' We were just feeling that good life, you know? And we go into the show, and they played 'High Time.' First time in so long. They never play that. We had already changed it on our sign, and that night everybody was like, 'Did you put it on there after you heard that?' "

Right now Amelia and Jeff live in Flagstaff, Arizona, but they soon want to move to Alaska. "We like the mountains," says Amelia. "Flagstaff is a pretty progressive place, a pretty hip town, but our goal is to get to Alaska where we can have our own garden and food and be more self-sufficient with the land. We're hoping to score teaching jobs up there two years from now."

High Thai
(serves 3 or 4)

Jeff and Amelia learned to make this from a Thai restaurant they frequent. They weren't taught by measurements, but rather a dash of this and a dash of that. Make it to your preference and let your taste buds be the judge!

13 oz. rice noodles (This can be purchased at a Chinese or Japanese market/grocery; Jeff and Amelia say that "for Pad Thai" will be printed on the package.)
Vegetable oil
2 tbs. sugar
2 tbs. vinegar
1 tsp. fresh lemon juice
1 tb. paprika
A dash of garlic powder
Various sliced vegetables. (They suggest broccoli, celery, carrots, and bean sprouts. They caution that sprouts can spoil easily on tour.)
Green onions, minced
1 1/2 tbs. fish sauce (For vegetarian sauce, this is a basic tamari-kelp-water mixture.)
1 1/2 tbs. oyster sauce (This can be found in imitation oyster flavor, made from mushrooms.)
3 or 4 dashes sriracha (A spicy chili sauce)

Soak the noodles for approximately 20 minutes. Strain, grab a handful of the noodles and begin to stir fry in a well-oiled pan or wok. Add the green onions, sugar, and vinegar. Mix well.
Next add the paprika and whatever vegetables you want to put in. Then add a dash of garlic powder, the fish sauce or vegetarian mixture, and then the oyster or mushroom sauce. Mix well. Add the lemon juice and the sriracha for that "kick that it needs." Cook to a soft consistency. The cooking time should be about 5–10 minutes. Enjoy!

Todd Goodno sits behind his table and a large stainless steel pot filled with Pesto Pasta. He and his girlfriend, Cheryl, are on their way to their summer jobs, but they've stopped in Seattle en route to see a few Dead shows, hang out, and sell their Pesto Pasta.

For the second summer in a row, they decided to travel to Alaska with their dog, Nazca, to work in a restaurant. The rest of the year, they live and work in Breckenridge, Colorado.

"I've been in Breckenridge for seven years," says Todd. "I want to try and make Alaska my home. It's so pretty. The mountains of Colorado are gorgeous and all but up there it's just so wide open, and there's so much wildlife, space, and land. Probably what Colorado was like 20 years ago."

After the summer is over, they will return to Colorado, where Todd is an electrician. "I've only been an electrician for eight months," he says. "It's fantastic. I'm just learning so much. It's a new trade, and something I can always do."

At the shows, the two decided to sell Pesto Pasta because they hadn't seen it done before. "It was different you know?" Todd remarks. "Because everyone's got pasta. Veggie Pasta, basic spaghetti stuff, but not many people have ever done pesto."

Todd says that he goes to Dead shows because he loves to be part of the scene, and hang out in it. "I love the music and it's a good lifestyle," he adds. "Hanging, making money, traveling. Instead of sitting at some job and doing it."

Pesto Pasta
(serves 4–6)

1 pound spinach garlic pasta	1 cup broccoli, diced
At least 1 1/2 cup packed fresh basil, finely minced	1/4 cup parsley, diced
	1/2 cup spinach
6–8 med. cloves fresh garlic, minced	1 medium zucchini, sliced
	Nutritional yeast, to taste
1/2 cup olive oil	1/2 cup walnuts, crushed

Todd points out, that the garlic, basil and olive oil are the main ingredients. "As long as there is a really basily, garlicky taste to it, that's what Pesto is all about," he says.

Mix together the basil, garlic and olive oil in a heavy skillet. Then, over medium-high heat, toss in the vegetables and sauté until the vegetables are cooked.

Cook the pasta, when it's done, toss with the pesto. Top with nutritional yeast, instead of parmesan, and sprinkle walnuts over the top.

Tenzig and Amity spend their days working on the farm they caretake ten hours a day, seven days a week. For them, cooking and vending at a Dead show is a vacation.

For some time, they have been caretaking land in southern Oregon. They farm apples, pears, prunes, raspberries, blackberries, and a ton of vegetables. They also have a quarter-acre organic garden on which they practice organic farming and crop rotation in hopes of maintaining the soil's fertility without the use of commercial pesticides. Working the land is something that they love and find spiritual.

At the '94 Eugene shows, they harvested fresh vegetables from their garden and made Super Chunk Pasta, a recipe that always changes with the produce that is ready in the garden.

"I have a hard time calling it work, because it's what I enjoy doing," says Amity. "Being close to the land, hard work, keeps you going," adds Tenzig. "Digging in the dirt, planting plants, taking care of the little babies in the greenhouse. Establishing a relationship with the vegetables you're taking care of."

The two take their fruits, vegetables, and cut and dried flowers to a farmers' market every week and try to get enough money to buy the things that they can't make or grow for themselves.

"Five o'clock in the morning before the farmers' market can be a little early," says Tenzig.

"But it sure can be fun," adds Amity.

"When you're working in the garden and growing your vegetables it really makes you feel good that you're doing it in accordance with nature and the rules that are involved in walking gently on mother earth," he says.

"You know where your food is coming from, you know what's been done to it," says Tenzig. "You love it. You love growing it, raising it from seed. There's a relationship. You feel that taking it out of the ground is what you're meant to do, that you're part of it. That unbroken chain.

"Gardening helps to remind you. It's when you tune in, when you really become conscious about what you're doing. It's just like wow, I'm putting in seeds, or harvesting, or all of a sudden, you tune into the river flowing by, or the birds, then you just stop what you're doing and look around and take it all in and stop to appreciate. We really need to appreciate things. It's a blessing. This moment is presenting itself as an opportunity to appreciate."

River Song Farm—Super Chunk Vegan Pasta
(serves 4–6)

"Always taste your food as much as possible, so you know what it's doing and to see how things blend, to taste herbs and to adjust," says Tenzig. "You have to taste it, you have to experience it along the stages of its cooking.

"For bringing it to eat at a show, you want to leave the vegetables on the crisp side, because you will be reheating it. Things seem to taste better when they sit for a while."

Although they made Super Chunk Pasta, Tenzig and Amity also made Buckwheat Banana Walnut Pancakes, French Toast, and Home Fries in the mornings at the Eugene shows.

Tenzig and Amity suggest cooking this near a garden where the vegetables came from.

1 pound pasta (They suggest using quinoa pasta or any other good pasta.)

Olive oil

5–7 medium cloves garlic, chopped

2 onions, chopped

3 carrots, chopped

1–2 cups water

1 cup celery, sliced on the diagonal or what ever else is artistic to you.

1 large zucchini, sliced in thick cubes

1/2 lb mushrooms, sliced

2 green peppers, sliced

1 cup olives, sliced

3 28-oz. cans whole peeled organic tomatoes

2 12-oz. cans organic tomato paste

Salt and pepper, to taste

1/4 cup tamari

1/2 cup dry red wine

Chives, to taste

2–3 tbs. lemon juice

Fresh herbs: oregano, thyme, rosemary, marjoram, to taste

Parmesan cheese

Tip: "If you buy your vegetables, wash them in a bucket, and scrub with a loofah. Leave soaking for 15–20 minutes."

Add these portions by eye, but try to be light on the rosemary and thyme. Using powdered or dried herbs will give different tastes.

Sauté the garlic and onions in olive oil. Add carrots and celery, as well as the herbs. Different vegetables should be cut in different sizes so that they can hold their shape throughout the cooking process.

→

After the carrots and celery have sautéed for a little while, and the onions are just turning tender, add tomatoes, tomato paste. Then add water, salt and pepper to taste. Substitute tamari for salt if desired.

Add green peppers, mushrooms, zucchini and olives. Let simmer for 4 hours on low heat. The longer simmering, the better.

At the end of cooking, pour in dry red wine and add chives. You may need to add a little lemon juice once it's stewing. Sometimes it will call for honey. Play with it, stir it all day so you're always tasting it.

When done cooking, get it into a cooler and under ice. Let it cool down first, but once it cools just above body temperature, ice it.

Boil the pasta al dente in lightly salted water with olive oil. Run cold water over it when done cooking which will stop it from cooking further. Top with the sauce.

Add parmesan cheese and fresh pepper grated on top. Enjoy.

Tim Koze loves to work with his hands, but working as a swimming instructor doesn't give much opportunity for manual labor. Whenever he goes to a Dead show Tim likes to make his celebrated "Tim's Sumptuous Stir-Fry," a dish which gets him cutting vegetables and working with his hands.

"I like stir-fry in that there is preparation and cutting," he explains. "I don't work with my hands unless I'm kinda fixing things. It's good to work with your hands, and with cooking, you have a closer connection to your food. It's not processed, and it says something about you. I think there's a lot more character in the manual work. You get better at cutting, too.

"I like cooking at shows because you're sitting there, cutting on a little table or cutting board and you see all kinds of things going on. Like just recently a drum circle started right next to where I was cooking. People come up and they'll want some stir-fry, and we'll barter things like beads."

When he wants to go to a show, Tim sometimes just makes his way over to Giants Stadium, which is forty minutes from his home in New Jersey. He also likes to go there to skate the massive inlay of concrete, a rollerblading heaven he just found out about.

"Giants Stadium is not very far at all, so I head up there," he says. "I've done three out of the last four years there, not necessarily because I like Giants Stadium, but it gives me another focus to take me from where I am. Giants Stadium is pretty crazy. I've had okay times there, it's usually just a more erratic crazy atmosphere."

Tim has been going to Dead shows since 1988, but remembers hearing their music when he was a kid.

"I was around thirteen when I found a bunch of my dad's old records in the attic," he explains. "One of them was

'Europe '72.' At first I listened to them a bit, and I was like, 'This is kinda countryish, but there's something that I like about it.' I guess what initially made me interested is that at Dead shows, people tend to be free. More able to express themselves rather than walking around, not saying anything and trying to look cool. Some concerts I've been to, people are just uptight about things.

"As I became more familiar with their songs, what they played and when, that added to the mystique. The fact they constantly toured and rotated their set list so that you could see them multiple times and have a different experience each time. I mean it's in the same context, it's still spontaneous and somewhat fluid. Plus, you would realize that there were people there for years and years just doing this and it made you more curious. Why had people chosen to leave whatever life they had in mainstream society to pursue this? You're participating in that, at least. Even if you're not living it, you're participating in it. It's perpetuating."

Tim's Sumptuous Stir-Fry
(serves 4 or more)

"This is a simple meal, that is aesthetically appealing and it's tasty," says Tim. "There's a lot more to stir-fry than meets the eye."

1/4 cup of olive, sesame, or peanut oil (Tim says vegetable oil doesn't work as well.)
Ginger, grated
7 carrots, cut in small strips
1 or 2 medium onions, sliced
Cauliflower (optional)
1 head broccoli
1 green pepper
1 red pepper
3 scallions, minced
1 1/2 cups bean sprouts

1 bunch of bok choy
3/4 cup pumpkin seeds, roasted
1/2 lb. firm tofu (cubed and marinated in the sauce takes on a great flavor.)
A few slices of tempeh, marinated in the sauce
Beans, any kind (which, Tim says, contributes to making the dish a complete protein)
Water chestnuts, canned or fresh
2 cups uncooked brown rice, makes 4–5 cups cooked rice

Needed: *A wok*

↓

SAUCE

"The sauce is where you add your personal touch to the recipe," he explains. "That is going to say 'You' when someone eats these veggies." But Tim doesn't cook the vegetables in the sauce because that can kill some of the vegetable taste. Make the sauce first so that the tofu cubes and tempeh slices can marinate for a while before cooking.

1 cup tamari
4 cloves or more of garlic
1/2 onion, minced
1 fresh-squeezed lemon

Fresh cilantro, minced
Corn starch or flour, to thicken the sauce
1 tb. hot or plain sesame seed oil

Vegetable Cutting Instructions: "Cut to your preference, just make them small enough so that they're going to stir-fry well," says Tim. "You don't want them to be too big, because it will be difficult to cook them evenly." Also, depending on price and what is available, Tim tries to buy organic produce.

Begin by coating the wok with oil. Add enough to cook all the vegetables, but don't saturate the vegetables you put in first. Grate some ginger into the oil. Add the vegetables in order listed. Start with the carrots, then throw in the onions. Sauté just until they become clear but don't let them caramelize. Cut the broccoli and cauliflower florets. Put them aside. Clean the broccoli stalks, dice, and add to the stir fry. Add the peppers, the scallions, and then the broccoli and cauliflower florets. Continue stir-frying throughout this process.

When the vegetables are tender but crisp, add the sprouts and bok choy. Top with the pumpkin seeds. (Roast the seeds in a dry wok first.) If you want to use tofu, marinate it in the sauce before beginning to stir fry. If you are using the tempeh or beans, throw them in now. Next add the water chestnuts. Stir fry for a while.

Start boiling the rice as you make the sauce.

Pour the sauce over all the veggies at the end. Premix and heat up if you like.

Serve the vegetables over cooked brown rice or throw the rice into the wok. But he points out that it looks fresher when you put the veggies over the rice.

Until he saw them in concert, Jeff Nordahl hated the Grateful Dead. Growing up in St. Louis, he was never exposed to the Dead's music or the scene surrounding them. Now he takes any opportunity to go to a show.

"I was into thrash metal; I thought that this was total wuss music," says Jeff. "I still am not into peace and love and all that, but I'm into the experience. I mean I'm still peaceful and loving, but I don't think you have to write it on your bus. It just comes along with the package."

Jeff works at a ski resort in Lake Tahoe and snowboards there every day. He is consistently amazed by the landscape. "I live right on a lake," says Jeff. "It's a Bob Ross painting every morning. The most unreal sunrises and sunsets you'll ever see."

Creation #68

(servings—whatever amount all your leftovers make)

Jeff suggests that when you're in the mood to experiment, take fresh vegetables and whatever is left over in the fridge and cook it up, but make sure that the veggies stay crisp. His only precaution? "Don't let them get gooey."

Zucchini, diced
Tomatoes, diced ("To get an appetizing red color," he says.)
Green peppers, diced
Apples, diced thin
Raisins, a handful
Fresh cashews (If you have the money to buy them.)

Onions, diced
Garlic, lots, minced or diced, to taste
Ginger, lots, grated and to taste
Red hot sauce, to taste
Cayenne pepper, to taste
Vegetable or olive oil

Because this recipe is based upon leftovers from the fridge, there really aren't specific amounts, just add whatever you want to use. First, sauté the spices, onions, garlic and ginger in oil. Add other vegetables according to hardness or however you would like to throw it together. Add raisins and cashews last. Sauté until ready to eat. Enjoy!

Jeff traveled to Oakland for the Chinese New Year shows, and made one of his many spontaneous dishes, namely Creation #68. "This was just Number Sixty-eight," says Jeff. "I've got twelve other ones that are so delicious. They're all like goulash, just a bunch of things thrown together."

Like many nocturnal chefs, Jeff's late-night inspired dishes take on various assorted flavorings.

"This is like recipe, late night feast #68 or so," he explains. "It's just a bunch of leftovers I had, zucchinis and apples and raisins and everything in the fridge. I came home, was watching *Mystery Science Theater 3000,* and was really hungry, so I threw everything together in a delicious mustard soy sauce, and some other goodness that I can't reveal. But it was really tasty and this is the final creation."

Sandwiches & Burgers

❋ ❋ ❋

When Brian Sonoskus takes time off from his job as a chef to see the Dead, he usually starts cooking. In fact, he likes to arrive at most Dead shows with a surplus of food to sell and give away.

"I love cooking and I get to come down here and do my work," says Brian. "It's good for interacting with people."

Before going to the spring 1994 shows in Phoenix, it had been almost eight months since Brian had been at a show, and he was beginning to crave the scene again. Traveling to the Arizona show from his home in Park City, Utah, he remembers that he found himself, "completely ecstatic just to get there. For three days, I've been bouncing," he says, smiling.

Brian and four friends traveled thirteen hours from Utah to get to Phoenix for the three-day run scheduled there. They originally planned to drive in Brian's blue-and-white Volkswagen bus, but the plan fell through. Like many older Volkswagens, it broke down before it even left Utah. "Old Volkswagens never die," explains Brian, "people just stop fixing them." For now, his is resting.

For the Phoenix shows Brian made his eternally evolving Fresh Hot Veggie Burger. "It's an interpretation," says Brian. "I've tried a couple of different recipes and it keeps evolving a little bit each time.

"Unfortunately, I didn't sell out of burgers, due to the excessive amount I made and having only one Coleman stove to cook on," he says. He also found it difficult to concentrate on cooking, because of the "work hindrance of the celebration of life going on both in and all around me."

Brian has been cooking all his life, both for fun and professionally. Cooking good quality food at Dead shows has become a way for Brian to offer his own contribution to the scene, something that brings him much joy. "Work has found a way to make me happy and occupy my time," he says. "I love the music, and all my friends are here. It's kinda like college gone on the road."

Like many Deadheads, he is passionate about hearing them play. "Its always been that feeling where I close my eyes and clench my fist, not in a rage of anger, but kind of a rage of orgasm."

Brian's Fresh Hot Veggie Burger
(Serves 6–8)

According to Brian, this recipe is an interpretation. He has tried a couple of different recipes, so it evolves a little each time. Brian maintains that burger leftovers make great chili! Just break up the burger to a clumpy consistency of texturized vegetable protein.

THE PATTY

2 cups cooked millet

1 cup cooked brown rice or 1 cup roasted, ground walnuts (depending on preference)

2 tsp. (about 2 cloves) fresh garlic, minced

1 cup (about 3) fresh carrots, shredded. (He says it makes for better presentation.)

1 cup wheat germ

1 cup ground, roasted sunflower seeds (Helps bind the patty together.)

2 tbs. *fresh* basil

1/2 cup pine nuts (or more), pureed very fine

2 tbs. honey

3 tbs. peanut butter (According to Brian, this helps take away the "grainy sawdust flavor of vegetarian food, and get some more of that childhood flavor." It also helps everything stick together.)

Salt and turmeric to taste

VEGAN HONEY MUSTARD DRESSING—adjust these measurements to taste if needed

5 tbs. Honey Dijon mustard

2 tbs. mayonnaise substitute

4 tbs. honey

1–2 tsps. tahini

Cook the millet and rice separately; grind the pine nuts and roasted sunflower seeds together with the garlic and carrots. Add the basil, honey, and peanut butter. At this point the batter will be very moist. If it is too moist, add more millet, if it's too dry, add more honey. Do this by eye and adjust by taste.

Next, form the mixture into patties. On a cookie sheet, bake them in the oven at 350 degrees for 30 to 35 minutes, until the patty is firm.

Put the patty on a bun, top with lettuce, tomato, and the Vegan Honey Mustard Dressing (although the burger will still taste great without the dressing). Play with the dressing. Make it to your taste.

Standing at the far end of the Shakedown during the Dead's 1994 three-day run in Phoenix, Arizona, the edge of the Desert Sky Arena is clearly in sight. But the fence surrounding the lawn prevents a full look at the stadium. Also impeding the view are hundreds of people who have begun climbing over the fence. It is Saturday night, and many more have shown up for the sold-out show than there are tickets available. Anyone raising their finger in the air or looking for a miracle is having a hard time getting into the show. The usual batch of counterfeit tickets haven't made it to the arena yet. As a result, there is a tense energy in the air, an air of impatience, frustration, and insistence to get inside and dance.

At first only a small group hangs around outside the fence, watching and waiting for the venue's security guards to look the other way so they can climb over. The next minute, it is chaos. The fence has been knocked down, and from a distance, it looks as if waves of tie-dye and bright colors are flowing over the wall, some running away from the mass of police and security guards who have rushed over to remedy the toppled fence.

And at the end of the Shakedown, the chaos continues, as people race from one end of the vending aisle to the fence and ultimately, inside the stadium. Many run past, itching to try and get over the fence to see a show in a place that the Dead have never played before.

Meeting Jim Brown, one gets the sense that he has been around the Dead scene long enough to know that this situation only means trouble. He shakes his head, acknowledging that this will likely be yet another venue in which the Dead will not be re-invited. Perhaps this is why he doesn't venture to shows anymore.

Jim estimates seeing between 100 and 150 shows in his lifetime. But he states that, "at the last number of shows I've been to, I've chosen not to go into the show." Maybe strange for a self-proclaimed Deadhead, but he has had close ties with the Dead scene since adolescence.

"When I was coming into my adulthood, it (the music and scene) was a way to get in touch with my feelings. To open myself to positive vibrations, positive feelings, love, caring, beauty, when there were very few environments in my childhood where that part of me was nurtured.

"It is a community that is supportive of my way of being, of what I have to offer materially in my food, and supportive of organic healthful eating habits. It's an opportunity to come together and to share information, experiences, creative energy."

Jim hangs out next to his big wheelbarrow full of food and drink that he has made for the occasion. They are organic, healthy, and really good. He sells apple pie, Vegan Organic Tofu Salad Sandwiches, and Herbal Rejuvenator tea.

Jim exists in a spiritual world. He is a monk, and with his dog, a black lab named Blessed One (Bless for short), he lives in a monastery in California. At the shows he practices different types of yoga. "This is karma yoga and bhakti yoga," he says pointing to the wheel-barrow full of food. "That's what this is. Bringing healthful food to people is part of that, but hatha yoga is my physical form." Originally, he went into a meditation center for the opportunity to live in a community. To practice deeply, to focus more in the support of a community.

Jim buys his ingredients from organic food co-ops as well as harvesting them from the earth. "From my farm, we harvested pounds and pounds of organic herbs which we used to make pesto for pasta at the Eugene shows," he adds. "We also harvested our lettuce beds for salad and our blueberries, raspberries, and strawberries for fruit smoothies.

"Cooking is a basic connection to the earth, and it's the way we see the energy that allows us to re-create our life."

Vegan Organic Tofu Salad Sandwich
(makes about 6 sandwiches)

This is a recipe which Jim says has evolved over the years. He composes the recipe at the produce market. Everything is in relation to the other ingredients. He mostly mixes and adds by eye. Add the amount of herbs, vegetables, and spices that you like. He suggests serving it as an open-faced sandwich on toast, stuffed into pita bread, or as a dip with vegetables. Those who have tried this at home have said that it is appealing to the eye, as well as the palate, and they love the variations in flavors and textures.

Needed: A blender

PESTO

		Salad Dressing
Fresh basil	Garlic, fresh	Olive oil
Oregano	Sea salt	Mustard
Rosemary		Red onion
Dill		Parsley
		Apple cider vinegar

TOFU MIXTURE

1/2 lb. Firm tofu	Curry spices: curry, coriander, cumin and turmeric—to taste	Lettuce
1 cup celery, sliced		Alfalfa sprouts
2 carrots, grated	Tamari, to taste	Powdered or prepared mustard
1 red onion, finely diced	Nutritional yeast, to taste	Multi-Grain Bread. Try it toasted.
Parsley	Cucumber, sliced	

Pesto: To make the pesto, combine the fresh basil, oregano, rosemary, dill, garlic, olive oil, and a little sea salt. Mix in a blender.

Salad Dressing: In a bowl, mix the olive oil and apple cider vinegar with the mustard. Add a little finely diced red onion and some parsley.

Tofu Mix: Drain the tofu, press it, mash it in a bowl. Put in equal parts diced celery, finely chopped red onion, and twice the amount of grated carrot. Add half the quantity of parsley as the celery and onion.

Once the tofu is mashed, the vegetables chopped and grated, and the dressing and pesto is prepared, you're ready to throw it together. To the mashed tofu, add the salad dressing and pesto. Toss in the curry spices—curry, coriander, cumin, and turmeric. Then add tamari to taste for a salty flavor and the nutritional yeast which gives the desired dryness. (It will tend to be very wet with all this.)

Spread on multi-grain bread, and add slices of cucumber, some lettuce and alfalfa sprouts.

Herbal Rejuvenator

Jim says that this recipe was born from "a long-time love of making sun tea and experimenting with making herbal coolers, using fresh organic herbs and fruit juices to make sort of a gourmet, healthful, herbal cooler that's sweet and energizing," he explains. "It is from the desire to have beverages that are healing, alternatives to the sugar carbonated, alcoholic, and caffeinated beverages which deplete the body's resources.

"You can mix and match different tea blends from boxes and make tea bags," he adds. "The dried herbs are impossible to get in organic and bulk. You can dry your own orange peel or get them in bulk, and vary the amounts to your own taste, or you can use herbal tea bags."

Hibiscus flowers	Cloves	Rosemary
Peppermint leaves	Cinnamon	Lemons
Chamomile flowers	Lemon grass	Ginger
Licorice root	Rosehips	Honey
Orange peel	Brewed with sunshine and	Orange and grapefruit juices
Spearmint leaves	spring water	

LEMON SYRUP:

Juice the lemons and grate half the lemon peels used to get a lemon zest. Drop them in water and let them soak overnight. Then add honey. "For example, if you are using 10 lemons, then use about two cups of honey. More or less depending on how sweet you want it. Add hot water, about the same amount as the honey. Don't let it be too hot, because the heat will damage the lemon juice. You just want to melt the honey so it breaks down and combines with the lemon juice." Put in fridge.

Chop the rosemary and ginger very fine. Add them and the other herbs into a large container. Squeeze the fresh orange and grapefruit last, then add in. You want to make sure you don't put too much lemon syrup in. If it's too sweet, adjust it. According to Jim, "The only way you can err is if there is an over powering citrus or honey flavor to it."

Pour boiling water over the tea bags or herbs. Let it steep for 10 minutes, then strain. Should cool down a bit first. Add the mixture to it by eye and by taste. Brew by making a sun tea. If you're in a warm place, put it in a glass and put it in the sunshine in the morning.

Tofu Avocado Sandwich
(serves 1)

2 slices of organic wheat bread
2 to 3 thin slices firm tofu
1/3 avocado, sliced thin
1 tb. tahini
3 tbs. fresh salsa (Greg suggests using one bought in bulk from a Co-op).
a handful of alfalfa sprouts (Greg only puts them on when he is vending at West Coast shows.)
A dash of tamari

Spread the tahini on one side of bread, and a dash of tamari on the other. Place sprouts on one side, and avocado on other. Put on the slice of tofu. Cover with a few tablespoons of fresh salsa.
Put slices together and munch.

Since the age of 18, Greg Lukens estimates that he has ventured to approximately 175 to 200 Grateful Dead and Jerry Garcia Band shows. In those years, accustomed to being at virtually every venue the Dead played, he made two kinds of homemade sandwiches to support his tour adventures. During summer tour, he sells Tofu Avocado Sandwiches and then makes Tempeh Sandwiches the rest of the time the Dead are on tour.

"They're two of my favorites," he says. "Usually during the summer I do tofu avocado because the avocado is in season and the other part of the year I do tempeh burgers. They're both unique in their own way. For me, cooking is very much a meditation. A good thing to focus on. It makes me feel like I'm giving a pretty good service and also providing myself with a living."

Meditation is an important part of Greg's life. It is also the reason why he likes listening to the Grateful Dead so much. Shows have become a meditation for him, a place to come in tune with himself, especially when he joins the myriad of dancers and spinners who inhabit the hallways during shows.

"Everyone has their own interpretation of the dance; for me it's a meditation," explains Greg. "For some, it is based on the Bible, like King David dancing in the Old Testament. Then for others, it's the high. A lot of times you feel like you're one with the music.

"To me, the Grateful Dead is really a myth in itself. What they stand for as far as the culture or subculture. There's a real sense of community and family on the road which you usually don't find in a normal, everyday setting."

Tempeh Burgers
(serves 4)

Tempeh, like yogurt, is a cultured food made by the controlled fermentation of soybeans. It has a nutty, mushroom flavor and a firm texture.

1 pkg. tempeh (He uses lemon grill or barbecued flavor which an be found in most co-ops.)
4 whole wheat rolls (Greg uses sprouted wheat because they're usually vegan.)
Sprouts and lettuce greens
Carrots, shredded or sliced thin

THE SAUCE (According to Greg, this is what makes this recipe unique. Add in any amounts of ingredients that you like, but be careful with the cayenne!)
3–4 tbs. crushed peanuts or peanut butter
1/8 cup tamari, or more, depending upon how salty you like it
1 tb. miso
1/2 fresh squeezed lemons
1/4 tsp. cayenne
1 medium clove garlic, minced
1/4 tsp. ginger, grated
Water to dilute

Slice the tempeh in half, horizontally, then again lengthwise (will make four square patties). Heat in oil in a skillet or grill them.
Then, to your eye, mix the peanut butter, tamari, miso, lemon juice, cayenne, garlic, ginger, and water into a spreadable sauce, and spread it on the sandwich. Add the sprouts, carrots and greens, and enjoy!

Heather and her boyfriend, Tim, sit on a blanket in the Washington, D.C., rain, cutting vegetables to make Veggie Pitas. It is their annual East Coast summer tour, and they do it almost every year. They especially like to be at RFK, since it is close to their home in Virginia and many of their friends go. At the shows, they almost always sell something, usually Veggie Pitas, a raw vegetable dish they make at home.

"I've been going to see the Dead since about 1985," says Tim. "It's just the best atmosphere I think is around. That's why I'll always come back every year."

"It's not so much the Dead, it's what you learn," adds Heather. "There are so many people here with common interests. You learn new things and you share with people."

When not at shows, Tim builds houses and Heather teaches ballroom and Latin-style dancing. She likes dancing for her job, but it's not as exciting as dancing at Dead shows. "It's mostly wealthy clientele, older," she maintains. "It's hard in a way, because you have to relate to a different level of people. I like what I do, but it's hard to relate to the people. They can't really know who I am, I can't wear my nose ring to work, I can't mention the Grateful Dead."

Tim and Heather plan on building their own house and farm in the next few years.

Heather is an avid gardener and is into growing organic food. Tim says that having the opportunity to build his own house will be an accomplishment, compared to the many houses he helps construct each year at his job.

"It makes me feel like that I can accomplish something," he explains. "With some people's work, you never see it. Like a bank teller or something like that. All you do is just get money and take it. Five years from now, what did they do for the past five years? Like in five years, I've built a few hundred houses. At least."

Veggie Pitas

Squash	Celery
Broccoli or cauliflower	Oregano
Sunflower seeds	Mushrooms
Parsley	Tomatoes
Carrots	Cucumbers
Radishes	Garlic powder
Green peppers	Whole wheat pitas
Wild onions	Salad dressing

Be creative with what you put into your pita. Use all of the ingredients, or add some of your own favorites.
Slice up all the vegetables, however you like to slice them and toss in a bowl with salad dressing. Stuff the vegetables into a whole-wheat pita. Sprinkle some garlic powder inside and add salad dressing on the side to dip the pita into.

When on Dead tour, Julie and Sandy like to make grilled-cheese sandwiches since the ingredients are easy to transport and they don't take up space in their small car. But they also make it to transform the traditional buttery, fat-laden sandwich into a healthier choice. On the 1994 East Coast summer tour, they grilled Honey Whole Wheat Grilled Cheese in olive oil and added tomatoes to create a more healthful sandwich.

"We don't use crappy white bread or nasty old butter," says Julie. "We use olive oil which is much better for you."

Julie and Sandy began the tour in Deer Creek, Indiana, and ended at the Giants Stadium shows in New Jersey. Originally from Vancouver, British Columbia, the two have been living in Key West, Florida, and have wanted to spend some time on Dead tour, but never had the chance.

"This is our first year seeing the Dead," explains Julie. "I like the whole hippie style. I guess we're all hippie wanna-be's from the sixties, but I like groovin' to the music!"

So far, Julie and Sandy have loved touring, traveling to different venues and running into the same people. For the same reason, the two plan on doing the fall tour or just general traveling outside of Canada and the U.S., to the Far East, Australia, and New Zealand. "I love seeing the world, learning, and meeting new people," says Julie.

Traveling with them during the summer, was Sandy's dog, Professor Peabody, who of course won't eat grilled cheese. "It's her first tour," says Sandy. "She first went to the show in Miami. She doesn't like it. There are too many people here, and it's too loud with the firecrackers. She likes it in the car."

Honey Whole Wheat Grilled Cheese with Tomato
(serves 1)

2 slices honey whole wheat bread
a few slices real Wisconsin cheddar cheese
1–2 "fatty" slices of real ripened tomato
Garlic salt, to taste
Olive oil

Between two slices of bread, place the cheese close, and grill in olive oil. Julie and Sandy suggest putting the tomatoes on last or the cheese will melt into it too much. Add the garlic salt. Close and flip until browned on both sides.

For years, Graham Parker lived his life on the road, going to Dead shows, and driving up and down the nation's highways. It was a time of freedom for him, but also a period in which he may have strayed too far from himself.

"Between 1984 and 1991, I didn't know anything but parking lots and the road," says Graham. "That's all I knew. Every day was a new thing. It was the freedom, the physical freedom, and going wherever you want to go. It was hard. Cash sometimes was real low, and then other times it was real high. Sometimes we stayed in the Hyatt, sometimes it was sleeping under a picnic table. But it was all fun." Then, for a while, he ran into trouble.

At length "Something clicked. My life just started getting better. I started taking care of some of my responsibilities, getting some old debts paid off. And I got a little spirituality in my life that I had always been searching for. I mean when I was out here, I'd do some good mushrooms and some good peyote and I'd get these real spiritual feelings, but when the trip was done, the spiritual feelings were gone. It was something that I was searching for, and I found that high while sober. That spirituality. And it's really cool, I really get off on it. Also, a lot of the things I only dreamed of doing are coming true in my life. Today I want it. Now I want it. My life's just got a better quality to it today.

"The funny thing about being sober is, you gotta want it. Needing it is one thing, wanting it is another. I see a lot of people who abuse the stuff and I did it for a long time too. Like these balloons [nitrous oxide], the people who get a balloon and then go right back in the back of the line, and by the time they're finished with that one, they have to form a line again, and just do that for hours and spend all their money doing it.

"When I got into trouble, I didn't think that the Dead was ever going to be part of my life again, but it's kinda like, you can take the boy away from the Dead, but you can't take the Dead away from the boy. You know what I mean? It's part of who I am today. It's just part of who I am. Period.

"I believe there are two emotions. Fear and love. You're either working out of fear, or you're working out of love. When I'm in these parking lots and inside the show, there's no fear whatsoever. I'm completely and naturally myself. I'm real comfortable around the people. A lot of open-minded people. People who aren't mean, people who aren't uptight. It's a good escape. A good release."

What has given Graham and thousands of other Deadheads support while in and outside the scene is the substance-free support group, The Wharf Rats. Formed by Deadheads to support themselves and others while around the Dead scene, they are most visible during the show's intermission when the group gathers for large and vocal meetings that are sometimes 200 and 300 people strong. It is a communing in which the whole Grateful Dead community is invited to participate. Graham, too, is active in the group and their meetings.

"There are a group of people who have been on tour, probably got in some trouble, and realized it was a result of the drugs and the alcohol that they were doing. This is a slippery place for anybody who is trying to stay clean, because there is so much around, I mean it's right here, it's right everywhere. We just are there for each other. We help each other, we give each other a safe place to be when we're at the shows. We're support for each other. We have a meeting at half-time and we put up posters at every entrance going inside, letting everybody know where we're at. We're loud when we have our meetings. We're loud as shit!

"We're trying to get a local chapter started in Virginia. When you're in recovery, and you're a Head, there's not a whole lot of them in your home town, so when you do find them, you all cling together. Last night we all hung together. There's about ten or twelve of us all from the same area. All old people too, all people who have been around for a while, so it was cool."

Phat Veggie Sandwiches
(however much you want to make)

Breads
Pita
Pumpernickel
Multi-grain
Whole wheat
White
7 grain
Cheeses
Muenster
Lorraine
Swiss
Veggies
Mashed avocado
Onion
Lettuce
Tomato
Shredded carrots

Cilantro
Clover sprouts, alfalfa sprouts, bean sprouts
Cucumber
Green Pepper
Nuts
Sunflower seeds
Crushed pistachio nuts
Sauces
Mayonnaise
Mustard
Thousand island
Oil & vinegar
French
Humous
Ranch
Creamy Italian

Choose any bread, add any sauce, cheese, nuts, and veggies. Enjoy!

Before Graham and his friend, Scott, went to the 1994 summer shows at RFK, they decided to make Phat Veggie Sandwiches, a literal smorgasbord of choices of veggies, toppings, breads, and cheese.

"I wanted to come and hang out in the parking lot, but I didn't want to be sitting still. And neither did Scott, so we decided to do something. To make some food. And we came up with this. We were both on tour before for quite a while and we knew what people liked. It's doing better than we thought it would. The attraction of seeing everything out, putting what you want on your sandwich. Getting what you want, rather than what somebody just made to sell. It's kind, man. It's like right on. People like it!

"This is doing so well though, we both have the itch to pick up and leave. I mean we're doing so well, we could stay in hotels every night. We were talking about it before, about possibly saving some money up and getting rent paid for a couple of months and go ahead and do it. We want to do some traveling, out to California. I want to go to Yosemite Park and stuff. I figure maybe in the spring and summer, we'll just jump on tour, and get back to traveling again."

Greg Bell sits on a milk crate in front of his van while stirring Nature Burger mix in a large wooden salad bowl. It is the second day of the Seattle shows, the ground has begun to dry from the rainfall the night before and the sun is actually shining. Greg wants to sell homemade French fries to go along with the Nature Burger he is vending, but is hesitant. He fears that if it starts raining again, water will get into the fryer's oil. He forgoes the potato stuff and stays with cooking just the Nature Burger.

For most of the summer '94 tour, Greg and his friend, Jim, intended to sell French fries, but ended up selling the Nature Burger on the side. As it turned out, they ended up selling more Nature Burgers than French fries.

"I think a lot of times the French fries don't sell by themselves, and you kinda have to do the McDonald's thing, and go, 'Would you like some fries with that?' Every time I say that, I feel like I'm working at McDonald's, at the drive-through!

"I like selling food, it's a little different than selling beer," he explains. "I used to sell it a lot, now everyone is selling it. It's an easy couple of bucks, so everyone has got a bunch of bottles they're selling. It's kinda like a flooded market." But he manages to sell some of the beer that sits on his make-shift table, though the Seattle parking-lot beer market is jam-packed, as are the garbage dumpsters.

Originally from California, Greg has been living in Colorado while taking classes at Colorado State University. He says that he hasn't

French Fries
(serves 2)

5 Potatoes, sliced in long strips
Soybean Oil

Slice the potatoes and cook in hot oil. Watch the temperature by eye, but you will need to mark the height of the oil, because if it gets too hot, it overflows. Just get it sizzling. Cook until brown. They also can bake well in the oven.

declared a major yet because he is interested in many subjects. But he doesn't always go to school.

"Sometimes I go to school, sometimes I work, and sometimes I don't do anything," he explains. "It just kinda depends on what I'm up to. I'm planning on going back to school next fall."

Since 1990, Greg has been touring and vending off and on. Traveling in his '77 Ford Econoline van with six other Deadheads was the first time he sold anything other than beer. He likes being on the road for the freedom to travel and thinks the shows offer an opportunity to do it cheaply.

"I think, initially, a lot of this is easy," he says. "You can travel not for free, but you can make money on the road. You can travel and work at the same time."

Nature Burger
(makes 2 burgers)

1 cup Nature Burger mix
Sprouts, a handful
Tomatoes, sliced
Onions, sliced
2 Rolls
Soybean oil

Prepare the Nature Burger according to package directions and to the quantity you want to make. "You pretty much mix it to your eye," says Greg. "It's a one-to-one. You can tell when you've mixed the water where it's supposed to be at." Form into patties and cook the burgers in soybean oil. Put on rolls and add slices of tomatoes, onions and sprouts. Top with ketchup, mustard, or any other favorite veggie burger toppings.

For a different burger, cook the nature burger in a skillet without forming into patties. Add tomato sauce and heat until browned. Serve on a roll with toppings.

The Kind Veggie Bagel
(serves 4)

Bagels (They use garlic, onion, poppy, sesame, or "everything" bagels.)
Cucumbers, sliced
Green peppers, sliced
Bean sprouts to taste
Vegan Recipe (This is a humous-and-avocado mix which will serve four.)
1 can garbonzo beans
4–5 tbs. or more tahini
Lemon juice—about 2–3 tbs.

Salt to taste
3 cloves or more fresh garlic
a handful of sprouts
1 avocado
2 or 3 green onions, diced small
A few sprigs fresh parsley, minced small
4 bagels

Blend or food-process the ingredients together and spread on both sides of a bagel. It will have a fairly smooth consistency. Top with the veggies.

NON-VEGAN RECIPE
1 cup cream cheese
1 avocado
1 medium clove garlic, minced
1–2 tbs. lemon juice (to keep the avocado from turning)

To your taste, mix the cream cheese, avocado, and fresh garlic together. Spread on the bagel, and top with the veggies.

On a number of tours, Tim and Meredith have been making and selling their Fatty Veggie Bagels, another culinary treat which has become a tour staple. Utilizing vegan and non-vegan bagel spreads, they are one of the growing number of vendors who like to offer vegan alternatives to Deadheads in the parking lots.

Selling a transportable item has provided them with the flexibility to walk around with the bagels in baskets, because when people are jam-packed and not moving through the Shakedown, mobility is key to vending.

Sometimes they change their offerings. At the '94 Eugene shows, in addition to bagels, they also sold Organic Peruvian, Colombian, and Guatemalan coffee and offered Rice soy milk as well as raw

sugar. Because it was a three-day camping event, people who desperately needed their coffee early in the morning were very happy.

92

Sludj" sits on a crate slicing tomatoes and avocados and spreading mayonnaise onto dark, rich, wheat bread. The temperature hasn't gone down much, but the hot Las Vegas sun has, so the preparation of the sandwiches isn't too strenuous. "Sludj" is making Veggie sandwiches to feed his love for good food cheaply.

"Howdy!" he greets a customer who walks up to the square two-car parking area where he sits. "You looking for a sandwich?" he asks. He makes another colorful sandwich with raw veggies for a hot, sweaty, and tired Deadhead. "It's a bummer, you don't get to play when you're vending," he says as he makes the sandwich. "But it pays off a certain amount later."

"I'm kinda a Deadhead," he remarks. "But I'm not really a Deadhead. I mean, I don't have any tattoos. But I love the Dead. I've been seeing shows for about three years, and I still don't remember hardly any of the songs they play. Like, if someone asks me what the set list was, if I don't have it written down, I can't remember any of the songs. I just like their music!"

"Sludj" lives in Salt Lake City, Utah, and in the summers spends his time going to shows and brewing beer. But in the winter he snowboards and enjoys the popularity of the ski resorts there. He pays for it all by vacuuming, making beds, and doing general maintenance at one of the local ski resorts in Salt Lake.

"I like the Dead because of the way it makes me feel, but I think it's more because of the people that are here, the sense of community. There's always going to be conflict, and there's always going to be problems in any kind of society. There is here, too, but at least the people are trying their hardest to really stand up for what they believe.

Psychedelic Veggie Sandwich

Honey whole wheat bread ("The bread is what makes the sandwiches," says "Sludj".)
Tomato, sliced
Green pepper, sliced
Red pepper, sliced
Avocado, sliced
Lettuce

Red onions, sliced
Cucumbers, sliced
Mushrooms, sliced
Cheese: jack, colby, provolone. ("Sludj" recommends using a cheese that is flavorful.)
Mayonnaise
Mustard

Place all the toppings and veggies on the bread. Eat and enjoy!

"What is nice is that I meet people with similar interests. I meet a lot of travelers. Just recently, I've been meeting a lot of people and getting to know people. A new world kinda opened up for me."

Mark Walcott's home is parked in front of a major cross-section of the Oakland Coliseum parking lot, where two Shakedown streets meet. During these busy Chinese New Year shows, people stream steadily by as he sits inside his bus buttering massive quantities of bread which he will use to make grilled cheese sandwiches.

Mark is a nomadic person. Living out of his house, a '71 red Volkswagen microbus, he keeps all his belongings, including a fishing pole, snow skis, and all the necessities for his traveling companion, his Shepherd-wolf mix, Marley.

Like many old Volkswagens, his often needs repairs. As a result, Mark sometimes gets stuck in one city longer than he wants, waiting for parts, money, or just hanging out too long.

"I break down a lot," he explains. "Boise, Idaho, is a good place to break down. Kind people, good VW places. I broke down on the side of the road and a guy pulled up behind me, saw my van, and gave me his number at work and told me if I couldn't get it fixed myself and needed help, to give him a call. I ended up needing a VW parts place, so I called him. He came and took me to a few VW places till I found the right one and he let me work on my van in his shop."

Unless the universe blesses him with a good-hearted passer-by, Mark sells grilled cheese to pay for the gas and parts for his traveling house. The savory fried sandwich is a tried-and-true traditional tour staple, as well as "an easy sure thing for gas money that everybody likes and trusts," he says. "There's nothing in it besides cheese and bread." But as he begins to grill, the venue security take away his Coleman propane stove.

A common problem for vendors is getting hassled by venue security. Concerned about enforcing vending rules, security works to keep vending to a minimum.

There has been a sometimes-fiery debate about the vendor presence on the scene. Many believe that vending leads to problems, which limits where the Dead can play. Others see the vending scene as a society which is integral to the Grateful Dead, as well as a thriving, magical subculture like none other. Mark, too, has had run-ins with the parking lot security at some venues where he has tried to vend.

"Sometimes it's a bitch because they won't let you have your stove out," he says. "They think you're going to blow the place up with one stove.

I like the music of the Grateful Dead, but I sure don't like their capitalist ways," he continues. "Twenty-five bucks for a ticket, no free shows, and then they hand me a piece of paper from the band saying that I can't sell anything because they want to make a deal with PepsiCo or something. What are they going to do, have Grateful Dead-merchandised grilled cheese and burritos? Get Pepsi and Taco Bell to sell burritos and Pepsis at a Taco Bell stand, so Pepsi can promote the Grateful Dead?"

Other than his distaste for the boardroom capitalism, which he believes may surround the Grateful Dead, he values the scene as a whole, and is perhaps thankful for its place.

"There are kind people here," he says. "No place else can you find this. It's the only place where you can have a pocketful of loose money and not have a problem. If you could get rid of the police and security it would be great."

Mark's Grilled Cheese Sandwich
(serves 1)

In the lots, Mark makes this in bulk, buying 30 loaves at a time. Although at times he uses wheat bread, he says that he uses any kind in the lot because, "most people just want a cheap sandwich for a buck."

2 slices wheat bread
1 tb. margarine or butter
A few slices real cheddar cheese

Butter each side of the bread. Add the cheese close, and cook on each side and flip often until browned.

The vehicles that Deadheads take to Dead shows are like no other mode of transportation in the universe. These assorted cars, trucks, and buses in their wild and colorful states are full of love and memories. Traveling in them is a joy for their owners and passengers, but they also lend proof to the perception that when the Dead come to town, a circus follows them.

They are sticker-covered, draped in dried wildflowers and sage, and at times, hand painted from bumper to bumper in every color imaginable. They are sometimes dilapidated, but never mistaken for anything other than a vehicle which is always on tour, even when the Dead aren't. Drivers have transformed these cars from a fiberglass-and-steel mode of transportation into a home. In their colorful splendor, they are a reminder to passengers inside and outside that they are members of a special traveling tribe.

The Volkswagen microbus is known to be the classic hippie car and there are enough of them on tour to prove it. Amilius, whose name means "Spark from the Light of God," has one of the more memorable

Sprouted Organic Humous
(serves 4–6)

2 cups garbonzo beans, dried (Amilius sprouts the garbonzo beans and blends them up in his bus.)
1 cup raw brown rice
1/4 cup tahini
1/4 cup lemon juice (or the fresh juice of 2 lemons)
4 cloves garlic, minced
3 tbs. olive oil
Herbs: dill, oregano, cayenne, thyme
Salt and pepper, to taste
Lettuce, tomato, or other assorted fresh veggies as toppings
4–6 whole-wheat pitas

In a large pot or bucket, soak about 2 cups dried garbonzo beans in water overnight. Drain in the morning. Keep the bucket tilted and rinse twice daily for about 3 days. When you see a small tail sprouting from the bean, it's ready to use. Rinse again, and add the beans and the other ingredients into a blender. While blending, cook the rice. When everything is prepared, stuff some of the humous mixture and rice into a whole wheat pita. Add lettuce, tomato and other veggies you like. Enjoy!

Volkswagens, and it fits his spirit. His 1979 forest-green Volkswagen bus is not just a home, it's also a traveling greenhouse. On the sides of the roof that he built onto the bus, he added circle shaped windows which let sunlight shine on the various plants, tapestries, and other necessities that make it a home.

"It's home. More than something that just drives. I grew up in Pennsylvania and Michigan, but I am from wherever I'm at, because this is my home," he says pointing to his microbus. "And wherever my home is, is where I'm at right now. The earth is home for all of us."

The bus is where Amilius meditates, cooks, and sprouts the garbonzo beans for the Sprouted Organic Humous Sandwiches that he sometimes sells.

Once a chef of egg rolls, grilled cheese, and other fried parking-lot delicacies, Amilius began making humous sandwiches because he felt it was important to sell healthy food, because that was what he was committed to eating himself.

For Amilius, meditation is a part of his daily routine and is in everything he does. Food preparation is one of the many meditations that he practices every day. He practices hatha and bhakti yoga in his journeys throughout the country.

"I've been traveling pretty much for four years straight," he says. "Occasionally I go to shows to sell food to keep me on the road." At one time Amilius was always on the road seeing the Dead, now he spends most of his time just experiencing, traveling, and occasionally going to a show to sell food and see friends. "I like the atmosphere in the parking lot and I see a lot of friends, but I've spent enough money on the Grateful Dead; it's time for other things."

Some of those other things, he explains, are learning about himself and the universe. "Traveling lets me experience all the lessons I need in life. Humbleness, respect, sharing, and faith in God, the supreme reality of the universe, the *is,* the *all!*"

The Burrito Chapter

❋ ❋ ❋

Two hours after the show's end, the Shakedown in the Eugene parking lot is raging. The scene has exploded. It is a camping venue and no one has to leave for the night. The advent of nightfall draws hundreds of people who have come just to see the scene. People are everywhere, buying jewelry, selling organic coffee, and bartering everything from pipes to juices. The scene, with it's sage, pot, and incense-filled air has become reminiscent of a Middle Eastern marketplace. The energy circling through the air makes this like no place else and adds to the mystique of the transient subculture that has just popped up in town. The sounds, also, are like no other concert parking lot.

So to hear someone shout, "Good Karma Burritos! Direct from the opera house, looks elegant in an evening dress, classy!" in a singing vocalization would not be considered unusual given the time and place in which it is yelled.

Because he gets tired of yelling out the usual Veggie Burrito chant, (i.e. "Kind Veggie Burritos, get 'em while they're hot!") Lionel likes to vary the advertisements that come flowing from his mouth, sometimes settling on a simple, "Curry burritos—they're the best damn thing you'll ever eat!"

"Sometimes I say, 'C'mon, Taco Bell is going be crowded!' " says Lionel. "We try to put a good feel to just selling them, instead of being like, *'Veggie Burritos!'* " he says, demonstrating by screaming in a loud raspy voice. "Just yelling out, or whatever. I think the whole thing is important from the start to the finish.

"That's the whole thing with giving something to somebody for a really good deal. The whole cooking process, putting a lot of good thought and energy into it and

then them getting it, and it being something they really enjoy. It's like a really giving back thing; it's something we really enjoy doing."

Good Karma Curry Burritos have been around the lot ever since their chefs Jake Newman and Lionel McCauley, began touring together in the spring of 1993. Since then they've gone on most every tour together, and can usually be found browsing co-ops and health-food stores around the country.

"When we do things together, it'll flow pretty decently. Especially cooking. It's something I think we do together really well," says Lionel.

"It does work out well," adds Jake. "When we sit down just to do simple things, like when we make them, there's a certain part of it that he always does, there's a certain part of it that I always do. He always puts the stuff on them, and then I always fold them, and wrap them, and put them in the foil."

"You always cut, and I always open," Lionel adds. "For a while I was cutting on the cutting board on the hood of the car, and little pieces of lettuce would fall off, and bake onto the hood, and Jake had a real problem with that." He laughs. "I'm like, I don't care, it's the outside of the car. Going down the road at sixty miles an hour, who cares if there's a little lettuce stuck to the hood?"

"You were not into that at all!" he laughs with Jake.

"I'm very anal about that for some reason," Jake laughs.

"We're very connected," Jake continues. "There are some people who have passed through my life, people who I've known before, people that I've known on tour. We're definitely connected together. There are just certain people in my life, who I think will always be there. With some people it just feels much stronger."

"And I believe that no matter what happens, all the unforeseen things that can happen, there's definitely connections that are greater," says Lionel. "They come from past lives, that are really much older than we are right now at this time. I've known Jake for five years, but that's not really how long I've known him. I definitely know that and believe that 100 percent."

Jake and Lionel love cooking, and especially making Good Karma Curry Burritos. "There's a connection being made, just us doing it, and to us putting our thoughts, and time and energy into what we're doing, and into the burritos," comments Lionel. "It's a whole process, what we're doing. I just think that stuff like that's important."

"And doing the best you can do," adds Jake. "I wouldn't want to sell something, I wouldn't want to give something to another person that I didn't feel good about, or that I wouldn't want to eat myself. I would just think to myself, 'Oh, this is just disgusting.' When somebody asks me, 'Are they good?' I feel very confident in saying, 'Yeah, I think they're really good.' "

Jake & Lionel's Good Karma Curry Burritos
(serves 4)

2 cups brown rice (raw)or 4 cups cooked
1 8-oz. can kernel corn
1 8-oz. can stewed tomatoes
1 8-oz. can pinto beans

2 tbs. curry (or more!)
1 clove garlic, minced
4–5 tortillas
1 large onion, diced thin
Salsa

According to package directions, bring the rice to boil in a large pot. Open the cans of corn and stewed tomatoes, drain off the juice, and add some of the juice to the pot. Boil together.

Once half of the moisture is cooked into the rice, add curry and garlic to the rice and mix well. When virtually all of the moisture is gone, add the corn, tomatoes, and beans. Keep stirring to distribute all of the ingredients evenly. The mixture should now be very soft and moist.

Lay out the tortilla shells. In the center of each, place a heaping spoonful of the rice mixture. Then top with onions and salsa. Fold and roll up the tortilla.

Make this dish with love! Enjoy!

Clad in his tie-dye apron, James Young and his Black Bean Burrito stove set-up can be seen and heard far across the parking lot at Cal Expo. Blasting from his brown Westfalia is a band that many Deadheads are beginning to follow around the country. It is the album *Picture of Nectar* by Phish. James stirs the black-bean-and-rice mixture to the music on a tall, green folding Coleman table and stove.

James and his wife, Cynthia, cook on tour as an alternative to staying home and working. To get to Cal Expo, they drove 2,200 miles from their home in Austin, Texas. They estimate that they will be driving a total of 20,000 miles throughout the tour.

"We like it," he says. "It's a lot more fun than sitting around, waiting tables, going to school or doing that whole 'I got a job, I can't do anything' sort of deal. It's great to travel. We went to all the national parks and everything. Yosemite, Grand Canyon, and it's like vacation, too. In between shows we go do stuff."

James started selling the Burritos, dubbed "The Best Black Bean Burritos in the World," during the 1993 summer tour. Though now he has a food service supply him with ingredients, many times they have had trouble finding them.

"We were in New York, and all we could find were black beans," he says. "We were like, 'Hell, we'll make it up.' It's a good thing, because they're a lot better. We used to sell refried beans, but they're too much of a Taco Bell sort of thing. I just don't like them that much."

James and Cynthia began dating and going to Dead shows together during the 1993 summer tour, around the same time that James began cooking the Burritos. Soon after that tour, they were married. Now Cynthia helps with the food but mainly tapes the shows while James stays in the lots and sells Burritos.

James remembers seeing his first show in 1988. "I just went in there, watched them jam, and I was like, 'Wow, this is what a show is!' I didn't know a single song. I have these 'seventy-four tapes that just make me want to go see the Dead, because I know that at least Jerry had it in him at one point. At one point, he could be the master. At least they still play better than most bands. Except Phish," he laughs.

The Best Black Bean Burrito in the World
(serves 4)

FILLING
1 cup long-grain white rice
2 cups cooked or 1 can black beans
3–6 medium cloves fresh garlic
2 or 3 tbs. sweet basil
Sea salt, to taste
2 tbs olive oil

TOPPINGS
4 12-inch tortilla shells
Monterey Jack cheese, shredded
Lettuce, shredded
Pico de gallo, homemade
Sour cream

PICO DE GALLO
3 fresh roman tomatoes diced chunky ("They don't get mushy and they're usually really red, which looks better," says James.)
2 yellow onions, diced chunky
1 jalapeno peppers, diced chunky
1/4 cup cilantro, minced
2 tbs. lemon juice
1 tb. vinegar

Start by boiling the rice. Add black beans, fresh-minced garlic, basil, sea salt, olive oil, and mix. Let the spices blend in. Put the mixture down the center of a 12-inch tortilla shell (natural, no animal ingredients) and roll up. Top with cheese, lettuce and pico de gallo. James tries to use organically grown ingredients.
To make the pico de gallo: Dice up the vegetables. Add cilantro, a little lemon juice, and a touch of vinegar to keep it preserved.

Embarking upon a Grateful Dead scene for the first time is without a doubt, an experience. The parking lot outside the show is at times chaotic, sometimes nerve-wracking but never unexciting. People from around the country and the world come to experience and share a part of themselves. It is an electrifying place and time, one that mainstream America knows very little about.

Brian Figueroa wanted to see what the whole "Grateful Dead thing" was about, so with a friend, he followed the band to three cities, beginning in Washington, D.C., at RFK Stadium. He sold Humous and Tabouli Burritos to support the venture.

"For me, it was to experience the whole concept of what this touring business is like, and the vending is kind of interesting to do," states Brian. "I was told that it would be a lot stranger to me and I would almost be blown away from the experience. I don't sense that at all. Everyone's backgrounds seems to be pretty varied."

Before the show, Brian had only been to one other concert. (He saw the groups Loverboy and Journey in high school). But he had listened to bootleg Dead tapes before he went to the show.

"I've listened to a lot of it, a lot of stuff I like. Some things I can't relate to. Like 'Space.' 'Space' is probably the most difficult thing for me to understand where that comes from. From an insider's point of view, I'm sure that that statement makes a lot of sense. I'm sure it's more enjoyable if you've had a couple of drinks or

Humous Burritos
(makes 4 Burritos)

1 1/2 cup chick peas	1/4 cup scallions
3 cloves fresh garlic	Black pepper and cayenne
1/2 tsp. salt	to taste
1/4 tsp. tamari	Organic tortillas
3 tbs. lemon juice	Sliced cucumbers and
3/4 cup tahini	tomatoes
1/4 cup parsley	

Soak the chick peas for an hour and a half, then boil them until soft. Mash and mix in the remaining ingredients. Wrap in an organic tortilla.

Top with sliced cucumbers and tomatoes. Wait until you're ready to eat before putting them on, or they'll get mushy.

something or if you're stoned. It would make sense at that point. I have no concept of what that is."

To get ready for the tour, Brian planned every detail, a stark difference from the lack-adaisical way that many Deadheads get ready for the road. He price-indexed the food they needed to buy for the burritos and prepared a precise recipe.

"Everything can be organized, and it makes things a lot easier," he maintains. "If every-thing is in a mess, you get confused about how to go about things. There's no way to get around it, it's just not going to work right. You're going to be running in eight different direc-tions to accomplish one task. If you lay everything out in the right direction then it won't be a problem."

Brian thinks that people are attracted to the Dead scene because of the common bond Deadheads have and because of their appreciation for the music. "They seem to be more open-minded than the general public," he adds.

"There are a lot of people, laying around the stadium, just listening, just to hear. It wasn't that important that they were inside," he explains, for the music can be heard from out-side RFK Stadium. "I guess they were comfortable just knowing that they were there, hanging out.

"Everybody said you've got to experience it at least once. So far, it seems okay. I mean it doesn't seem like anything out of the ordinary. Nobody seems that weird."

Tabouli Burritos
(makes 6–8 servings)

1 cup bulghar wheat
1 1/2 tsp. salt
1/4 cup lemon juice
1 1/2 tsp. garlic
1/2 cup scallions
1/2 tsp. mint leaves
1/2 cup chick peas

1 1/2 cup green peppers, diced
1 cup parsley, minced
Black pepper to taste
2 medium tomatoes, sliced
1 large cucumber, sliced
Organic tortillas

Soak the wheat for 15 minutes in 1 1/2 cups of boiling water. Drain any excess water if needed. In the order listed, add the remaining ingredients.
Mix together and let chill.
Wrap in an organic tortilla and top with tomatoes and cucumber.
Brian suggests you play around with this recipe to your taste. "You don't have to stick to the directions," he explains.

There are many people who see the Dead scene as a family, a global connection which numbers in the millions. People from all over the world come to see the band, then unify into a traveling circus, forming a close network of family and friends. The Dead family atmosphere is closely connected to another family that holds many of the same values and ideals, one which is not centered on following the Grateful Dead, but rather on people coming together.

The Rainbow Family is a coalition of people throughout the world who focus their energies on caring for one another and making their world a better place.

Rainbow Gatherings are the times when the Rainbow Family meet. The event is well known and loved among Deadheads. It is a time to join with others, Deadheads and non-Deadheads, in a nature-centered, organized, and communal way. A Rainbow Gathering has come to be known as an assemblage of people from all over the world who want to share ideas, skills, and visions.

Following the first Rainbow Gathering in 1972, the events continue to be publicized by word of mouth. Their whereabouts are always known on Dead tour, for many Deadheads will stop off at the gatherings as they travel across the country.

Dragon and Willow can often be found on Dead tour, but spend more time in the Rainbow community, and at times make the gatherings their homes.

"We spread it wide everywhere," explains Willow. "There is a lot of family on tour. One of the main reasons we're here is to generate funds for the gathering. A lot of people have respect for us on the lot when we do that. We pretty much take around a donation can or a hat and generate funds that way. People come up to us and go, 'Wow, are you guys the people who are doing the free kitchen? Here, here's some money,' or 'I remember you guys.' I'm sure Jerry knows who we are, too. I hope so."

"It (the burritos and pasta) started out as a free kitchen, but things haven't really been going the way we planned," says Dragon. "We do free food once in a while, and we always give it away whenever somebody is hungry. We usually just ask for donations, but some of the food we sell for a straight price. We're doing the whole East Coast tour, but we try not to plan anything, we try not to make any foundations. We're going to be doing Kentucky Rainbow Gathering right after tour, though. Cumberland regional, it's a real high gathering."

"It all started back in the summer of 1972," explains Willow. "There were street families who decided that people should start gathering in the forest and pray for world peace, and heal the mother. People went to our first National which was up in Paonia, north Colorado. There was barely any publicity about it, but 25,000 people showed up. That's when our first circle of consensus started. That's when the family gets together and forms a consensus on what needs to be done, what needs to be bought and how to go about it safely."

"The gatherings are a month-long including seed camp. The seed camp and clean-up is when we leave no trace, and go around and seed everything and rake it over. We save twenty percent of the magic hat money for that. If it's re-seeded right, you'll see no trace of us in a month. Usually we'll make a place look a whole lot better than when we first got there."

Willow, which means Elf, and Dragon, whose name is connected to Agni Dragon, have been going to gatherings for years.

"Two years ago I was in Colorado for the National and it was in the very same spot where

Rainbow Vegan Burritos
(makes 6–8 Burritos or however much you want to make!)

2 tomatoes, diced
1 red pepper, diced
2 onions, diced
2 carrots, shredded
1/2 small head red cabbage, shredded
1/2 small green cabbage, shredded
1 jalapeno, sliced
8–10 cloves fresh garlic, minced
3 cups of either red, dark red, and white kidney beans, black beans, and lima beans
2 cups raw brown rice
17 spices ("Our special thing," they say. "It's really high, you can feel it in back of your throat for hours. It's really hot, very spicy, and it gets you sweatin'.") Try—cayenne, paprika, black pepper, curry, basil
Tortillas

Cook the rice and fill a tortilla with it—and lots of the above veggies. If you use beans, pre-cook them. Roll up the tortilla, and enjoy!

"They are live burritos, live food," says Dragon. "Everything is raw except the rice and that the beans are pre-cooked because we don't have time to soak them," explains Willow. "Everything is live, and by not cooking it, everything is medicinal."

Rainbow Pasta

1 pound pasta, any kind
Tomato sauce
3 fresh tomatoes, diced
Vegetables ("Any kind that
    you can get your Rainbow
    or Deadhead hands on.")
2 green peppers, diced
1 red pepper, diced
1 onion, diced

Lots of fresh garlic ("Very
    medicinal.")
17 special herbs and spices
    (At home add in lots of
    herbs and spices.
    Unfortunately, their spice
    recipe is secret.) Try
    cayenne, paprika, black
    pepper, curry, basil.

In a pot, combine the tomato sauce, spices, and vegetables
and let simmer for a few hours.
Cook the pasta al dente, pour the sauce over the pasta, and
serve.

the very first gathering ever was and it was so beautiful. Nine thousand six hundred thirty feet high, I mean really high. So beautiful. My favorite gathering to date. There was something like forty kitchens, two CALMs (Centers for Alternative Living Medicine), twenty-two tea kitchens, a kiddy village, where all the nursing mothers take the children, and where pregnant sisters go when they want peace and quiet. There's activities for the kids. It's kinda like a work-shop for children, and for people who want to have children.

"Each year, we have twenty-three regionals and one National. We also have council, Thanksgiving council and spring council where we decide where the next National is going to be. I've done two of those. The last one was in Alabama. It's going to be up in the mountains of Montana this year. Scout family council. The family chooses at least five people to do the scouting. They drive from state to state getting topographical maps and they decide the best places for the gathering depending on how many springs there are, how much vegetation is edible, and how many streams there are. The whole reason for us doing this is to find the best place where the family could actually settle down for the rest of their lives. That's what we're looking to do, and to spread light."

Following their birth as a band in 1965, the Dead began taking their carnival-of-sorts on the road. Back then, fans would largely find tickets, rides to the shows and other touring essentials through friends, signs, and by word of mouth. Three decades later, the information superhighway, the cyberage, has given Deadheads an opportunity to connect with other Dead fans and plug into the Dead scene, twenty-four hours a day.

And now there are a variety of ways to do it over the computer. Grateful Dead bulletin boards can easily be found while roaming through the world of the Internet, connecting with smaller Deadhead bulletin boards, or dropping in on the San Francisco based "on-line community" and computer conferencing system, The Well.

In addition to megabyte upon megabyte of Grateful Dead-related banter, users can get information related to lodging and camping, traveling tips and directions to shows. But users also buy and sell tickets, discuss songs, and trade tapes over the system. Now, hundreds of thousands of Deadheads, many of whom are college students, utilize this as a valuable Grateful Dead information resource.

"I like the convenience of being able to talk to someone anywhere in the country almost instantaneously and for free," says one "Nethead," Naomi Berner. "The B-boards (bulletin boards) have a lot of information on them that would be hard to get elsewhere. It's easier to check the B-board for updated tour dates than to call the hotline every day. For what I need, the Internet is fast, easy, convenient, and free."

The board that Naomi logs onto is rec.music.dead, an extremely active board which hosts around 75,000 users. The board is heavy in on-screen computer language. The lack of human emotion is made up with happy symbols like :):):). Thus Deadheads can still manage to retain a feeling of closeness and understanding.

Naomi, an economics major at Carnegie-Mellon University in Pittsburgh, is one of thousands of electronic spirits who log on daily to read what the Grateful Dead masses have to say. It has also helped with finding a ride to shows. Four months before she was to leave for the '93 shows in Las Vegas, her car died. As the shows got closer without a mode of transportation, she was determined to go on the West Coast tour. She sent a message to the board asking if anyone needed a rider and offered to pitch in for gas. Five days before she was to leave she found a ride. Once Naomi found transportation, she realized that she would have to generate enough cash to go on tour, so she did some research.

"When I decided to go on tour, I realized I'd have to make money on the road since I was starting out with only $200 dollars or so. So I looked around a bit for burrito recipes that were vegetarian. I needed to make burritos that could be made with minimal facilities. I took some of those recipes and created ten or twelve sample burritos using various vegetables and different types of beans."

She chose one, which turned out to be Easy-to-Make No-Cook Burritos. "It's a much different recipe than most other burrito vendors," says Naomi. "But dozens of people have told me they're great, and they're really easy to make on the road."

It was a dish which financed the whole tour and all the sightseeing she did in-between. "I saw all the shows (except Detroit), never was shut out of a show, never wrote home for money, and never had to get miracled," she says.

"Seeing the Dead lets me see a great band five times a week and also the entire United States," she says, referring to seeing the Grand Canyon, San Francisco, and Wyoming while on tour last summer. "It gave me a built-in itinerary, and I was able to pay for it all. I was never stressed, even when cash was low or when ticket prospects were dim, and every day was a different adventure."

No-Cook Veggie Burritos
(makes 5)

"These burritos will keep for approximately fifteen hours without refrigeration, but try to keep them out of direct sunlight if it's really hot outside," says Naomi.

"You can adjust this recipe to your taste," she adds. "I've experimented while I was in different areas of the country and used local veggies including chopped green peppers, corn, tomatoes, and cucumbers. Don't be afraid to eliminate one vegetable and substitute another. They're good to prepare in the morning and then take to the show or a ballgame, for lunch or dinner. They won't spoil until the next morning!"

5 burrito-sized flour tortillas
1 can refried beans
1/4 of a 16-oz. bag of frozen mixed vegetables
1/3 head lettuce, shredded
1/2 yellow onion (red is good, too), chopped finely
1 stalk celery, finely chopped

1/4 lb. fresh bean sprouts
Spices to taste (try low-salt Cajun blend—"Watch out for some mixes that are too salty.")
Taco sauce

Lay each tortilla out on a square of tinfoil. Open the refried beans and stir them well to mix the oil sitting on top. Spoon out a heaping spoonful and spread it down the center of the tortilla, leaving room on the sides and a bit on the bottom to fold the tortilla up. Finish the can with all 5 burritos. Next, sprinkle 1 to 2 tbs. of the onion and celery over the beans on each tortilla. Rinse the frozen vegetables in lukewarm water just until the frost is gone. "No need to cook them," says Naomi. Sprinkle a handful of vegetables over the beans until all the vegetables are gone. Season to taste. Then pile a handful each of the lettuce and bean sprouts on the burritos.

Fold the burritos as follows: Fold the bottom up and then the sides inward. Wrap the burrito in the foil the same way and you're ready to go to the show!

"When you serve them, pour on taco sauce and munch away!" exclaims Naomi. She used to hand out individual packets of Taco Bell taco sauce when she was on tour, but the store-bought kind is fine.

Naomi suggests that the burritos sit for an hour or so before serving. This gives the vegetables a chance to defrost and for the spices to blend in.

In 1987, Ken Jamititus moved to Utah from the East Coast to enjoy the skiing that the state is famous for. Now he loves living there for the horseback riding, in-line skating, and water sports.

"I moved to Utah seven years ago for the skiing," says Ken. "I knew that it was going to great. But after my first summer, I realized that the summers are a whole lot more fun, because Utah is just a big outdoor playground. Now, it's wind surfing, rollerblading, mountain biking. I haven't really rock climbed yet because you can only get into so many sports in depth."

Ken is a believer that people should live life, be active, and take every opportunity to use their bodies.

"The human body is basically the same as it was ten thousand years ago," he explains. "It was designed to be worked hard every day, and modern-day society has made it so you don't have to do that to survive. You don't have to run for your food and all that fun stuff we had to do back when we just grunted and groaned at each other. I kinda like to do what my body is supposed to do. Plus it's a whole lot more fun than settling down. In the summertime it's tough between sailing, blading, and mountain biking, and I try to juggle those three. But in the spring, I always end up going to the Dead shows. It's kinda like my part time job between my real jobs."

Ken last traveled to his "job" with friends from Utah to see the 1994 shows in Vegas. To support the venture, they sold Stir-Fry Burritos. "We first made them in Cal Expo," he says. "The last night of Cal Expo, people were coming back for seconds and thirds and friends were coming for it. They really liked the taste. I've just always been a firm believer that you can make anything that anybody else makes. What's going to make it special is the sauce. Sauces are key to good food."

Ken loves going to see the Dead and being a part of the tribe that follows them. "They're awesome musicians for one thing," he says. "They've got a great environment that follows them wherever they go. It's probably the best vacation from mainstream America that you can get. Everybody is in a good mood, everybody is mellow, nobody is uptight. It's just all 'thank you's' and 'pleases' and it's not brown-nosing. No bullshit. Even though there are ten different people on this block that are selling food, and it is technically somewhat competitive, there is no competitive attitude. It's more communal."

During the winter, Ken works for a limousine company that services the Snowbird ski resort, and in the summer he instructs rollerblade skating, though he could be using his degree as a mechanical engineer from New Jersey Institute of Technology.

"I've got a mechanical engineering degree that I've chosen not to use," he explains. "I can't stand office politics, I hate bullshit, and I hate swallowing other people's bullshit because they're my superior. So instead of dealing with the frustration of watching things done stupidly, I kinda just choose to stay in an environment that I have more control over. Which basically means, if I ever got a real job, I'd probably get my ass canned."

Polynesian Stir-Fry Burritos
(serves 4–6)

FILLING
1/2 cup water chestnuts
1 cup of 2 types of pea pods (your choice)
1 carrot, sliced
2 onions, sliced
1 parsnip, sliced
1 green pepper, sliced
A few tbs. or more to taste pine nuts and/or peanuts
Fresh cilantro, minced, to taste

POLYNESIAN SAUCE
1/4 cup soy sauce
Water
1 tsp. brown sugar
Assorted spices—Try basil, oregano or whatever you like to use
1 clove fresh garlic, minced
Fresh-picked ginger, a few slices
4–6 tortillas
Peanut oil

Begin by stir-frying the veggies in peanut oil for about a minute. In a separate bowl, mix, then toss in the Polynesian sauce. Stir and add the pine nuts or peanuts as soon as veggies are done.
"Sprinkle fresh cilantro in there and get a nice, warm, soft tortilla. Put a big scoop of the veggies into the tortilla, fold it up, wrap a paper towel around, and you're ready to stuff your face," says Ken. "No plate. It's finger food."

113

In the last ten years, the image of a Deadhead holding up a tinfoil-clad burrito while yelling out, "Kynd Veggie Burritos—get 'em while they're hot!" has become a familiar sight in the parking lot.

The Ultimate Burrito
(serves 4–5)

FILLING
1 cup raw brown rice
1/2 cup tomato sauce—make it fresh or buy it if you don't have time
1 cup dry black beans

Vegetables, any kind, diced
Paprika—to taste
Garlic powder—to taste
Onion powder—to taste

TOPPINGS
1 cup black olives, sliced
1 jalapeno, diced
Salsa

SALSA (Wendy and her friend Beth spend four hours each day making the salsa with every fresh vegetable they can possibly throw in.)

3 fresh roma tomatoes, diced
1 onion, diced
1 green pepper, diced
Tons of cilantro
1 jalapeno, diced
1 fresh squeezed lime
4–5 cloves fresh garlic, minced
Whole wheat tortillas
Tortilla chips on the side

Cook the rice in 1 1/2 cups water. When the water and rice come to a boil, turn down the heat and add the 1/4 cup tomato sauce, vegetables, paprika, garlic powder and onion powder. Let simmer until cooked. This will make a Spanish rice. Add beans and let simmer.
Load the filling into a whole-wheat tortilla, and top with salsa, olives, and jalapenos.

Burritos are a popular dish to sell on tour because they're easy to prepare and easy to double the initial investment. Amongst the plethora of these burrito enterprises, Wendy's "Giant Burrito" is one of the few that offers a vegan alternative.

Originally an equal partner in the Stylin' Fat Veggie Pizza business (with Elijah), Wendy stopped making pizza so she could create her own vegan dish for tour.

"Obviously they're (the pizza) the hottest item in the parking lot," said Wendy. "I gave it up because it didn't fit with what I felt what's right and what's wrong. If I wanted to be a food vendor, then obviously it had to be vegan."

She then started cooking Rasta Pasta, a fresh pasta dish which, though popular, was difficult to cook in bulk on the road. Now she has settled into the role of providing the Giant Burrito, a recipe that she has changed around to ensure its non-dairy appeal to all food tastes in the parking lot.

"It had to be vegan so I was limited in terms of what I could put in there," she explains. "I tried to be creative with everything I put in. I wanted to tell people who I know are vegan, 'You come here and be sure that I wouldn't let anything related to any animal product near this food.' "

A significant part of Wendy's cooking is presentation. The countertop on which she prepares and sells the burritos is cut to hold containers of fresh salsa, olives, and jalapenos, so customers can see how she prepares the food.

"I like people to see what goes into it. That's the whole thing with the burritos as far as I'm concerned," she says. "Obviously the food has to taste good and I try to present it so that anything I do, whether the pizza or the pasta, is fat food. I want to give people the feeling that they got what they paid for."

Cooking on tour since 1990, Wendy is still a dedicated Dead fan and loves the society which forms around the band. "People come here in their crazy contraptions from all over the country, people that you might not see except on Dead tour," she explains. "And they all end up in the same place and form a little city. It's a great thing. A phenomenon, basically. I wish the greater population could look at it that way.

"Where else could this happen? Who cares if these people happen to party and have long hair. Who cares? Just look at it from another aspect. It's young entrepreneurs who are truly happy doing what they're doing."

In one of the many Shakedown aisles at the 1994 Oakland Chinese New Year shows, the Flyin' Burrito Circus' tarp is set up from the back of a modified Dodge Winnebago. Covering the back door is a purple, white, red, and green tie-dyed sheet. With candles, incense, and a propane lamp burning beneath, it is a parking lot home. In the background, Bob Marley sings from a stereo, as the familiar smell of sage and sautéing vegetables wafts through the air from the truck. It is an aesthetically pleasing place to buy burritos. After all, the group's motto is, "It's not just a Burrito, it's a way of life!"

The Flyin' Burrito Circus is a group of people who are eager to follow a peaceful way of life, one that other Deadheads dream of as well. They dream of living on beautiful land, growing food and sharing with other people with similar interests, values, and ideas. Like the commune, the idea is to find a place on which people can live together and reap the benefits of community living.

The Flyin' Burrito Circus have begun the project, "Land for the People." The grassroots, non-profit group say that their aim is to "purchase land on which we can live in peace with ourselves and others in an environment we create as a society of individuals who wish to unite and live together."

The Burrito Circus' plan is to generate money to buy land. Festivals and gatherings can be held on this space for the purpose of raising more money to purchase more land for more people who want to live this life.

Serge Sunshine Hack is one of the organizers of the effort. If he isn't at a Dead show or traveling, he gathers mailing lists and tries to organize people to work on the project. So far he has found someone to harness solar energy for the bands that will play at the festivals. He is currently searching for land on which to begin the process.

"If all I do is get this idea out and someone else does it, then great," explains Serge. "It's one thing to have a good time with your life, but to create a full lifestyle for a lot of people, then that's something bigger than yourself."

The Flyin' Burrito Circus' Hot Veggie Burrito
(serves 4)

FILLING
1 cup Pinto beans
Cumin, to taste
1 cup raw Brown rice
1 cup Black beans
Tortillas

TOPPINGS:
Lettuce and tomatoes
Sour cream
Cheese, whichever kind you prefer,
  shredded

SALSA
Tomato sauce from 1 small can (about 16 oz.)
4 fat tomatoes, crushed
1/4 cup yellow onions, diced
2 or 3 green onions, diced
Cilantro, minced to taste
2 to 3 cloves fresh garlic, minced
Ginger
Cumin

Cayenne pepper
Black pepper
fresh lemon and lime to keep the salsa
  and lettuce fresh
Red wine vinegar, to taste
Lemon juice, to taste

To make the salsa, mix diced yellow and green onions and tomatoes in a bowl. Add cilantro, fresh garlic, cumin, ginger, cayenne pepper, and black pepper. Add lemon juice to keep the mixture fresh.

Cook the brown rice and add black and pinto beans to the mixture. Heat and mix well. Place a heaping amount down the center of the tortilla and roll up like an enchilada. Do this with a few of them until you fill a casserole dish. Bake at 325∞ for 10–15 minutes (or until cooked). Add the cheese on top just before it's done. Then separate each and serve. Add plenty of salsa, top with lettuce and tomato. Add other toppings you like! Enjoy with love!

Beverages

✳ ✳ ✳

Matt Hauser and Kristina Moore sit behind a small table covered with bottles of syrup flavorings, paper cups, a coffee grinder and an occasional splatter of dark brown coffee grinds. Parked behind them is their Volkswagen bus. Painted in bright colors, the side spells the word, "MIRACLES," in red, blue, and yellow.

It is the second day of the Eugene shows and Matt and Kristina are taking a break from working. During the fall of 1994, they opened Miracles Cafe, a place which offers vegetarian food, assorted coffees and teas, and a place for local artists to showcase their music, art, and poetry.

The idea began when they moved to Bellingham, Washington, and into a house which had previously been a cafe. "We saw all these people walking by all the time going to campus, parking in front of the house, and so we said, 'Let's open a cafe!' " explains Kristina. "We just started from the ground up, slowly but surely. We used recycled wood and paint and everyone would just bring us things. One brought us a coffee machine."

And so the building became Miracles, a sunny shop, complete with cats, dogs, and lots of people. Located one block away from Western Washington University, students go to eat, drink coffee, and just hang out. But people also come for the music. Bands inside and outside the cafe play anything from rock, punk, violin, to guitar, two or three days a week.

"I love it," Kristina says. "Right now, it's a lot of hard work, but it's gonna pay off. You meet a lot of really neat people, and you're always enjoying yourself because it's for yourself and you're doing a service for everybody else. People come daily to help us out, give us ideas, paint. A lot of the painting on the bus is from people stopping by and adding on. We make it everybody's place to be."

All the coffee at Miracles in Bellingham and at their remote parking-lot location in Eugene is freshly ground. Matt and Kristina take care in choosing where their beans come from, conscious of their purchases' economic effects.

"We did a lot of research before we actually opened," Kristina says. "I met about fifty different roasters, went to their places, they showed me their beans, how they roasted it, where they got their coffee. The espresso beans we use come from places where they don't take jobs away from other countries. That was one thing we were concerned about."

With all the work it took to get Miracles together, they wanted to take a break and travel to see the Dead. When the band played in Eugene, Matt and Kristina went on the road, and Miracles came with them, in the form of an espresso maker, syrup flavorings, coffee beans, all in a colorful '71 Volkswagen pop-top camper. Once at the shows, they sold espresso, Italian soda, tea, cafe latte, mocha coffee with fresh grated chocolate, as well as hazelnut, vanilla, almond, amaretto, raspberry, and lime syrup flavorings.

"It's nice to see so many people together as a unity and a community," she says about the scene. "You just feel free, you can walk and talk, no one feels threatened, or scared. It's not like how society is now. It's like you're own little secret society. You feel safe, you don't have to lock your doors."

"Hey, do you have any iced coffee?" a woman inquires approaching the table.

"It's wonderful," Kristin continues while making the coffee. "Great to be able to camp in the same spot. I think this is the only place where you can do that. It's so much easier."

Miracles Latte

2 tbs. freshly ground espresso beans
1 cup chilled milk
Flavored syrups, a dash or two

Needed: An espresso maker

Take the porta-filter (which is the spoon-handle in which the grounds go) and pack it tight with the grounds. Stick it into the machine.

Pull the shot of espresso. Kristina says that it should come out into a nice, creamy brown color. Pour into a cup and add in syrup flavoring, if desired. Take some milk (however much you like to use). Steam until it gets a nice froth on top. Take a spoon and separate the milk from the froth. Pour the milk into the cup and then spoon the froth on top.

Kristina and Matt suggest making an Iced Latte in the summer. Just add ice!

Miracles Magic Italian Soda
(serves 1)

1 small shot glass full of *syrup* (This is a sugar syrup with a flavor extract. It can now be found in most grocery stores in the coffee section where it is sold in smaller bottles. Matt and Kristina use the brand Torani. Try making your own syrup by experimenting with juices, fruits, herbs, and sugar or honey.)

Ice

8 oz. Seltzer water

In a small shot glass, fill the syrup halfway up. If you like it extra sweet, pour it in all the way up to the top. Play around with the flavor that you like.

Pour in the ice, the flavor syrup, and then the seltzer into a glass. Matt suggests putting whipped cream on top. At the cafe, they stick straws in to "get a nice drink out of the whole thing."

A neophyte to the Dead scene would undoubtedly be surprised at the enormous amount of cooking that goes on in the parking lots of a Grateful Dead show. Ovens, stoves, deep fryers, ice makers, and blenders are used to cook anything and everything. There aren't electrical outlets in the parking lots, so vendors have had to be creative in providing energy for their appliances.

The majority of vendors use propane and some use generators, but there are a few that use the sun. To blend his Fresh Fruit Smoothies in the parking lot, Chris Kulina does just that. He uses solar energy to power two industrial blenders in which he whips up his fruit-and-ice concoction.

"I live up in Northern California and solar energy is really big up there," says Chris. "One of my friends does a (fruit) shake booth at fairs and he runs blenders off solar energy. That was the idea that got us into it."

So for two years in a row, he borrowed his friend's blenders and solar equipment and went on the road with the Smoothies. There usually are no problems with it unless it's too cloudy to charge the batteries.

The equipment he brings to collect sunlight can be involved. "We use two sixty-watt panels and four deep-cycle batteries," he explains. "Assuming that there's a full base of sun, batteries can be kept relatively charged by having the panels hooked up." Chris also utilizes a 1,500-watt inverter, a box that converts DC battery electricity to AC household current (110 volts).

"It's fun to go to the shows and do something that's different that shows off solar energy. A lot of people come around and just ask about the system. You can easily point to the solar panel that's hooked off the truck, point to the batteries and the inverter and show how the system works. That's kinda neat."

Chris has sold the Smoothies at about twelve shows, yet has seen upwards of seventy-five concerts since attending his first show at the Worcester Centrum in Massachusetts in 1985.

"When I started going to shows we used to take our little camp stove and just hang out and tailgate in the parking lot and make our own food," he says. "Now, doing the fruit shakes is just a nice way to be able to do tour and not worry about money, hang out, and have a good time. You always meet people coming by. It's work, but when the days are good, it pays off."

When not at shows, Chris restores Volkswagens. For the last ten years he has repaired the ever-popular classic Deadhead vehicle. "I've seen some creative things done," he says about Deadheads who convert their buses into traveling houses. "Being on tour and seeing some of the things that are making it puts a lot of faith in Volkswagens. It'll always get you there. I've seen more packed VW's going farther on nothing than any other vehicle."

Fresh Fruit Smoothie
(servings depend upon the size of the blender you use)

The secret, Chris says, is blending everything very smooth. "Using a really powerful blender and using the honey enhances the power of the fruit," says Chris. For the Smoothies he made at the Vegas shows, Chris used a 1,000-watt, industrial-size blender. At home, put it on the highest setting.

"Play it by ear to make it taste good," he explains. "If it's hot out, add more water to make it last longer. Honey brings out the flavor, but it doesn't work as well with strawberries and raspberries. Too much honey doesn't taste good." He suggests using honey if you prepare this with frozen fruit. Chris tries to use fresh fruit whenever possible, and for the shows, he hauled all the spring water he used from a well in California.

Ice
Honey (How much depends on the fruit, and its sweetness.)
Fruit (He has used blueberries, strawberries, raspberries, peaches, bananas, cherries.
He suggests not using any citrus fruits.)
Milk or spring water (Depending on whether it will be vegan or not.)

Needed: A blender
This recipe will be made according to the size of your blender. Into the blender, pour in about 1/2 an inch of honey. Put in one banana (or other assorted fruit). Then add ice so that 1/2–2/3 of the blender is full. Then add more fruit. Pour in milk (use water if vegan) until the ingredients fill 3/4 of the blender. Top off with ice depending on the thickness you want. Blend up and serve.

Going on tour with the Grateful Dead can be a vacation from life. Responsibilities are few and the adventures are many. What is important is getting to the next show and finding enough capital to make it there. Aside from gathering vending supplies and possibly calling home once in a while, there's not much to worry about.

Kristen Cady thought so, too. In June of 1994 she graduated from the University of Maryland with a B.S. in animal science and pre-veterinary studies. As soon as she graduated, she took off to the West Coast for her own vacation. To go on tour.

"I'm kinda taking the summer to not even think about it," Kristen says. "This was the light at the end of my tunnel so I'm just enjoying it. I'm not worried about anything."

Except for moving to San Francisco after the tour ended. Kristen went right from graduation to touring, so all of her belongings were left in Maryland. "My stuff is boxed up at my parents' house, waiting for the end of tour so I can go home and move it to San Francisco."

But her school career isn't over yet. While in the Bay area, Kristen will have to take physics and bio-chemistry to complete the requirements for veterinary school.

On the tour, Kristen supported herself in a number of ways, one of which was vending Strawberry Lemonade at the shows in Eugene.

Although she was going to make regular lemonade, her friend, Silvana, who she travels with and who sells guacamole and chips, suggested that

Home-Made Strawberry Lemonade
(serves 6–8)

8 cups water
1 cup fresh-cut strawberries
1 cup frozen strawberries
Honey and sugar to taste
1 cup lemon juice
2 lemons, sliced

In a large container, combine 4 cups of water and the fresh and frozen strawberries. Let soak in the sun for 3–4 hours.
In another container, combine the lemon juice, sliced lemons, and water. Chill for 3–4 hours to let the lemon juices soak through.
Mix the two containers together and add honey and sugar to taste.
Serve chilled over ice.

she make Indian Strawberry Water.

"I made the lemonade because it was hot, and I wanted something besides beer for people to drink," Kristen declares. "I thought it was going to be hotter than it was. Last year, in August, it was unbearably hot here, like Cal Expo-show hot. I wanted something that would refresh people without being alcoholic."

Kristen thinks that she will always be involved in the Grateful Dead community. "It's a part of society that I fit into," she explains. "Some people are in the working field, some people do their business. I guess I feel best in this part of society. But I can still do what I always intended on doing with my life. I just have my fun differently.

"I think that the younger people here are attracted to the freedom, and people in general come because of the power that they (the Dead) possess," she adds. "Just the energy that is created, that everyone knows is there. It's interpreted differently by each individual. I think that people who have never been to shows can't understand without experiencing it."

Herbal Smart Drink
(However much you get after boiling down)

To learn more about herbs with healing properties, Nathan suggests reading up on herbs. Perhaps start off with an easy guide, like The Way of Herbs, by Michael Tierra (Pocket Books, 1990 edition).

Gota kola: "This opens blood vessels and arteries and so it increases blood flow throughout the body, especially in the brain," says Nathan. "It's good for circulation and purifying the blood."

Gingko: "Increases and speeds up the synapses in your brain. So literally you think faster."

Licorice Root: "A stimulant. It also increases blood flow, it's good for the muscles, and aids in digesting and respiratory functions."

Pau d'arco: "Good for the circulatory and the respiratory system."

Ephedra: "A stimulant. Ephedrine is derived from it. This is a bronchial dilator."

Rose Hips: full of vitamin C

Vitamin C: Good for the immune system

Boil the herbs into a super-concentrated tea. Cook it out 3 times by filling up a pot half-full with the tea. Then fill the pot halfway with water. Boil it down. Pour it out through a strainer and do it two more times.

"It's better to take in a tea than to take it in a tincture, because in tea everything is pulled out of the plant itself through grain alcohol. Grain alcohol sucks all the nutrients and everything out of the herbs," he explains.

All-Natural Smart Drink, catch a buzz!" yells Kim over and over in a musical tone. She is sitting in a remote parking lot at the Phoenix shows next to a cooler full of herbal all-natural tea. A virtual blend of neural activity, the Smart Drink is designed to propel its drinker into the realm of a natural high. She and her boyfriend Nathan concocted the drink which contains Gota kola, an herb which speeds up the thought process, Ephedra which increases the blood flow, and licorice which aids the digestive and respiratory circulation systems.

Nathan has learned to utilize herbs, spices, and food to heal himself. He views food as a drug, an organic mood-altering material, which can be an aphrodisiac or a depressant. "Depending on the ingredient, food is a natural mood- and mind-altering substance," he says.

"Different foods give you different feelings," explains Nathan. "Broccoli is a downer. Spinach and alfalfa are a stimulant. It matters what you eat and it depends on what your moods are. Food is a drug."

Nathan learned about changing physical and emotional states with herbs and food from culinary school and working in a juice bar. He has put his food knowledge to use in making the "Smart Drink," and claims that the concoction is, "a buzz in itself."

Nathan, who has seen seventy or eighty shows since he was thirteen, describes himself through his unusual hobbies. He is a self-professed escape artist, contortionist, magician, juggler, fire breather, gymnast, and gourmet vegetarian chef, and adds that Kim likes to call him an evil clown or an emperor.

Doing more than just breaking out of things, Nathan explores the risky side to life, and sees his escape-artist hobby as a means to break out of the confines that "hold us all back in life.

"I've always been kinda claustrophobic and am the kind of person who wants to overcome my fears," says Nathan. "That's why I'm an escape artist. That's why I'm a cliff diver, too. I was afraid of heights at one time. I overcame it by jumping off cliffs. If you face something that you're scared of, you'll eventually overcome it and get better at doing it."

Chris Boyd and Kyle Anderson stand in the hot Sacramento sun, shirtless and wearing reflective sunglasses. They resemble the stereotypical tanned, young California Deadhead, but as they periodically yell out, "Psychedelic Fruit Punch, Hunch Punch, two dollars a glass!" you hear a sharp Southern drawl.

Best friends since high school, the two traveled from Georgia to go on Dead tour as well as a tour of their own. Their only goals on the 1994 West Coast summer tour was to travel through, "scenic zones of the country," and to follow the Dead.

"When I'm in places like Bryce Canyon with scenic beauty around, it takes me away from a society that has gotten out of control lately with its concrete buildings and monetary basis for everything. That's when I'm at peace and I feel that traveling is a spiritual experience," says Kyle.

During the tour, Chris and Kyle sold burritos, beer, spaghetti, and bundled sage, but they primarily sold the Psychedelic Fruit Bob, an alcoholic drink drenched with fresh fruits—peaches, red and green apples, kiwis, oranges, strawberries, grapes, plums, and pineapple. It is a recipe they developed in high school.

"It's something we used to make when we were back home. We would go to parties and make Hunch Punch, with golden grain, several other liquids, and lots of fruits," remembers Kyle. "That's what it was called there, but we're calling it several things here. We're going to change it each day. Right now, it's like an Apple Bob. You go bobbin' for apples! Today it's the Psychedelic Fruit Bob."

Kyle thinks people go to shows to get away from society. "It's probably because of the absence of social constraints, and many people probably think that they can be themselves in this arena." Chris also believes that people come for "the atmosphere," and that local crowd comes "just to see what's going on. I dig the following," he says. "The mass behind the band. I like their message."

Chris and Kyle did the tour in a small truck with another rider they picked up along the way. They plan to tour again, but want to do it in a bigger vehicle.

"We hope to equip ourselves with a better ride to come do this again. We're kinda cramped right now in a little tiny truck. We want to get back home and get something mobile, like a mobile home. Something that's better equipped for life on the road."

Psychedelic Fruit Bobs

1 part 190 proof grain alcohol (Everclear)
1 part rum (Bacardi)
1 part vodka (Smirnoff)
Peaches
Apples (green and red)
Kiwi
Oranges
Strawberries
Grapes
Plums
Pineapple
Hawaiian Punch, Kool-Aid, or Hi-C
Pineapple juice

Slice the fruit and mix with the alcohol and fruit juices. Chris and Kyle say that the secret is to let it soak overnight, so that the fruit absorbs the alcohol. "In addition to having an alcoholic juice, you have an alcoholic fruit which is tasty, so it kinda hides some of the bite that the alcohol can have," says Chris. Leave the fruit in the punch and serve some in each glass.

The alcohol to use? "We could have bought cheap liquors, but we decided not to, because we like to have a product we can stand behind and give someone somethin' good," they explain. Mix in whatever you like. Enjoy!

129

Golden Devotion Potion, Alabama Gatorade, Rippleade, Friend of the Lemon, and Uncle John's Band Lemonade sound like some names that a fast-food corporation might conjure up if they tried their hands marketing Grateful Dead–inspired food and drink. Or they could just resemble a potential mock setlist for an Dead April Fool's Day show. Yet these are just some of the names that Adam Gordon and friends came up with to sell Adam's fresh mint Lemonade.

Although he has been vending at shows since 1991, the 1994 East Coast summer tour was the first year that he sold Golden Devotion Potion. After a period of vending egg rolls, Adam found it was easier to vend Lemonade. He sold seventeen gallons of the drink at the shows in Highgate, Vermont.

"I decided to switch out of egg rolls because it was too laborious," he explains. "This is a lot easier. The whole labor-intensive process, except squeezing lemons, gets kinda messy, and if you have any cuts on your hands, it's painful.

"I came up with the recipe from working at two restaurants in Maine," he adds. "I just sorta messed around with lemons, sugar, water, mint leaves, and stuff like that. I talked to different people, I talked to people at the restaurant, where they used to make fresh-squeezed lemonade. Basically, I did it to taste."

When not at shows, Adam waits tables at home in Maine and majors in environmental studies at Bates College. Until he graduates, he plans on catching as many shows as possible.

Adam thinks that the Dead's mystique has to do with present-day society longing to experience the Age of Aquarius again. "It's the last haven of the sixties," he says of the scene. "It's a mobile metropolis, it's always different. It's a city. It's got a Main Street."

"I like the Dead for a couple of reasons," he explains. "The spirit of the crowd during shows, the fact that no one sits down, the fact that you can just dance crazy and be completely uninhibited by the people around you because they're doing the same thing. I also like it because it's a culture shock. I love culture shocks and I don't get enough of them. White-bread America has been all too banal or just boring. At a show, every-thing's really different but somehow everyone fits in."

Golden Devotion Potion
(makes 4–6 servings)

2 quarts mountain spring water
9 lemons, freshly squeezed
3/4–1 cup cane sugar (or more to taste)
A generous handful of organic mint leaves
Garnish with a lemon wedge and strawberry
1/2 cup grapes, crushed & pureed

Optional: 4 or so drops of peppermint or spearmint extract

Fill the container three-quarters full with mountain spring water, fill the rest with ice. Add all the ingredients, mix well, and enjoy! When the container is empty, crush the grapes down for a grape puree.

Dead shows that are scheduled on the East Coast in the early spring are infamous for throwing Deadheads a load of cold, wet, snowy, gray weather. Perhaps this inspires the Dead to play their favorite bad-weather tune, "Cold Rain and Snow," at this chilly time of year.

As usual, the spring weather for the 1994 Nassau Coliseum shows was bleak. Rain poured on many of the days that the band played the Long Island arena. To counter the effects of the wet-cold environment, Cherise Rafilk and friends sold hot chocolate from the back of their bus.

"We sold it because it was cold, and I didn't see many people selling hot chocolate yesterday," she maintains. "I usually sell clothes, but the cops are taking stuff. I was afraid they would make me put my things away and I wouldn't make any money."

When the weather is nice and there are fewer police hassles, Cherise likes to make and sell dresses, overalls, and pullovers. "I usually shop a lot for material," she explains. "I go to regular fabric stores, and look for stuff that's out of season to buy for the next season. I really want to work with hemp, but I haven't been able to yet. Otherwise, I like to work with cotton."

Cherise, her boyfriend, Karl, their dog, Bolt (who can skateboard) and four friends from their home in Milwaukee, Wisconsin, traveled the 1994 East Coast spring tour in Karl's 1966 forest-green Volkswagen Microbus. Depending on the weather and how much money they had, they stayed in the bus or found floor space in a hotel room. Though she loved it, she says that touring with so many people in one vehicle can be problematic.

"I don't like having all the clutter around," she laments. "You'll want to do something, but you can't because you've got like four people to go through. You've got a bunch of different personalities to deal with, and one person has a problem and it's everybody's problem. Well, when you've got six people, there are a lot of problems. But I like it because you get closer to people at the same time. You get all the family and all the love

Cherise's Rainy Day Hot Chocolate
(serves 1)

1–2 tbs. hot chocolate mix
1 cup water
Whipped cream, to taste

Prepare the hot chocolate according to package directions. Add whipped cream. Enjoy on a cold-rain-and-snow sort of day.

and everything, but it's hard cause there's a lot of stuff to deal with in a small area."

Cherise's first show was in Chicago in 1992 and she continues to thrive on being a part of the scene. "I like the music, I like the scene, I like the way people live. It's a small tribe," she says. "I don't like the cops and scalpers, and I don't like when you can't vend stuff. I like the people, and the traveling, but I like seeing shows most of all."

Through its twenty-three windows, Quinn Kalisch's '72 Ford van is illuminated with sunlight as the afternoon Seattle sun goes down in another Grateful Dead parking lot. Two parking spots away, an orange Volkswagen bus is being raffled off by its owner and a crowd gathers around. The spectacle brings a steady flow of customers towards the back of Quinn's van where he is juicing fresh carrot juice and grinding live wheat grass into juice.

"There are so many things in this world that are destructive. Juicing is something that you can do everyday that's life-giving, and it's tapped into that life-giving energy," he explains. "I've been caught up in a lot of destructive things in the past, and this is a real easy, ritualistic way of keeping tapped into food, tapped into life-energy."

According to Quinn, the wheat grass is full of chlorophyll, which brings oxygen to the red blood cells. "It increases oxygen," he says. "Chlorophyll itself is a rush, it's a stimulant. Basically, it's the only thing that could be considered a whole food. It has all the basic nutrients, minerals, and vitamins in it. It's the most live thing you're putting in your body.

"It's healthy and it makes you feel good. Since I've been juicing, I've noticed that when I go back to eating something kinda funky, I get these feelings back, emotions and feelings and anger coming into me. Juicing just keeps your emotions really straight."

Juicing is also what he does for a living. An avid juicer, Quinn lives in Seattle and works at a coffee and juice shop called Ed's Juice and Java. There he began juicing, something which has helped him make positive changes in himself and his environment.

"I'm definitely ready to blow out of here and be out in the country and get to some area where there is more room to spread out," he says. "For me, to stay in touch with myself, I need to be surrounded by a lot of mountains and oceans and trees. Any kind of nature, really. It's almost a tease in Seattle, because you can see Mount Rainier and you can see the Sound, and you can see the beautiful areas, but there's this city barrier. It's only half an hour away, but it's such a hard drive to get there."

Deadheads who have never seen wheat grass juiced before are amazed as he cuts the grass from the fifteen or so small potted wheat grass plants that sit upon the counter inside his van. As soon as he cuts the plants, he jostles them into a wheat grass grinder which extracts the juice to make the energy-giving drink.

"I think it's just important, because you go to the Dead shows, and everyone is drinking beer and getting really high, and doing all sorts of funky things and this is a really inexpensive, quick way of getting something really healthy into your body."

Green and Orange Live Juice

1 pound organic carrots; yields 8 oz.
1 cup wheat grass; yields 1 shot glass full.

Needed: A wheat grass juicer and a regular vegetable and fruit juicer. The wheat grass needs a separate juicer. If the carrots are not organic, soak them in water with a little lemon and a little salt. This, Quinn says, helps to remove the chemicals.

"When it's juiced, the nutrients in wheat grass die after three minutes. Be sure to drink right after you juice it. The same is true with carrot and vegetable juice. A lot of the nutrients die, so keep it iced. It's still good for you, but you're going to lose a lot of the nutrients."

"I have a really hard time trying to sell anything," he explains. "My friends were selling grilled cheese sandwiches in Sacramento, and I kinda said I'd help them out just because I was with them. I felt so weird about selling grilled cheese. I almost felt like saying, 'Don't eat this, it's bad for you!' But selling the juice, I don't really feel like I'm selling stuff. I still do a bit, but like when people come up, they're so psyched. They're just going, 'Yeah, got my fix, man, my juice!' so it's a lot more than just selling."

Waking up with the early morning sun, your body is exhausted from the show the night before. You lay prone, trying to sleep in a tent that is far too hot as it sits in the sun. Once up and walking around on the dewy grass, the heat doesn't seem so bad. Your friends and assorted other Deadheads in the campground who crashed around the fire pit the night before have come together to wake up with a cup of coffee or espresso.

If you're fortunate enough to camp next to Jonathan Edwards, the coffee or espresso portion of the morning could really happen in your campground. For some time, Jonathan has been selling coffee and espresso at shows as well as in the campgrounds where he stays, meeting people and making conversation.

"Well, I've always wanted an espresso after a show and in the morning before a show, and I figured that others would, too," he explains. "It also is a good way to meet folks. I do the vending not to make the money, but to meet the folks. I've met most of my good friends on tour by just vending. I can't make a killing or anything, and that's not the purpose. It's just to meet folks."

Jonathan makes his Joe with a coffee and espresso maker that he plugs into the socket of his '84 Mazda 626, a vehicle which boasts license plates that says, "GARCIYA" with a "STEAL YOUR FACE" sticker in the middle. Though he usually gives it away, when he needs the money he'll sell large cups of coffee and espresso for one dollar, fifty cents for refills and $1.50 for doubles. He says that he doesn't really stick to the prices. "I take change if that's all that folks have and I trade for juice, milk, etc."

"Drinking coffee is a conversation enhancer," he observes. "What beats sitting down the morning after (the show) and sharing coffee with some folks you've just met? I also like to see folks wake up after drinking my coffee. They get a whole new outlook on life. It's a legal stimulant."

Cosmic Coffee and Espresso
(serves 2)

4 tbs. beans for 2 cups coffee

1/4 cup beans for 2 double servings of espresso

Coffee beans (Jonathan suggests that you use real fresh ground beans from a coffee shop.)

Spring water—2 cups for 2 cups of coffee. 1 cup for 2 double servings of espresso.

Cream and sugar

Needed: A coffee or espresso maker

Measure out the beans, grind them, and depending on whether you're making coffee or espresso, alter the amounts. Put in about twice as much for espresso. The beans should be ground very fine. For espresso, he doubles the beans and uses less water. Jonathan suggests using spring or bottled water.

"The main thing is not to use tap water and to use tender loving care," says Jonathan.

Jonathan loves touring because he gets to see the Dead and travel. "Well, there's the open road and the show that lies at the end of the road," he explains. "I like the freedom from my everyday routine. I get antsy sometimes being cooped up in the same town, doing the same things with the same people day in and day out. When that bug gets me, it's time to hit the road.

"When I first went to see the Dead, I was amazed by the family and the togetherness. That's what first struck me, and then the music really pulled me in. It's like a family reunion of sorts. I see folks on tour that I only see on tour and we get together and dance to some great music, enjoy the scene, enjoy the tunes. It's a spiritual revival, I guess."

Jonathan's Mom's Very Veggie Vegetable Tour Soup
(don't follow it exactly—should serve 8)

According to Jonathan, this is adapted from a recipe that he borrowed from "dear old mom. It is great to take on tour," says Jonathan. "Cook it ahead of time and let cool. Pour in Tupperware containers and freeze. Carry it on tour in a cooler. If you keep it on ice, it can last a week or longer!

"I usually munch on this after a show," he says. "About two hours before I go to a show, I take it out of the cooler and let it defrost. After the show, just heat it up and enjoy!

1 16-oz. bag of frozen mixed vegetables
1 cup potatoes, diced (though sometimes he uses much more)
1 cup onions, diced
1 1/2 tbs. of sugar
1/3 cup soy sauce
3 1/2 cups V-8 juice (Jonathan recommends V-8. "I've tried others," he says. "It doesn't come out right.")
10-oz. can tomato soup
28-oz. can diced tomatoes
1 tsp. salt
1/2 tsp. pepper
1/2 head of garlic, chopped fine
1 tsp. basil
1 bay leaf

Put all ingredients in a 5 to 8 quart stock pot. Add about 1 or 2 quarts of water, or until all the vegetables are covered. Simmer for 1 to 1 1/2 hours. Stir occasionally.

Jonathan says that you can substitute fresh veggies for frozen ones. "What I usually do is use a combination of frozen and fresh. I throw in fresh green, red, and yellow peppers, mushrooms, carrots, and other veggies that are in the fridge." Be creative!

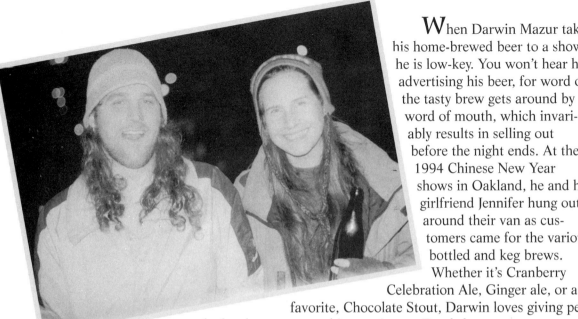

When Darwin Mazur takes his home-brewed beer to a show, he is low-key. You won't hear him advertising his beer, for word of the tasty brew gets around by word of mouth, which invariably results in selling out before the night ends. At the 1994 Chinese New Year shows in Oakland, he and his girlfriend Jennifer hung out around their van as customers came for the various bottled and keg brews.

Whether it's Cranberry Celebration Ale, Ginger ale, or a favorite, Chocolate Stout, Darwin loves giving people the chance to taste his creations at Dead shows.

"I just like the idea of meeting people and having them try the beer and getting all the compliments. It feels good," he remarks. "I'll usually split the beer with another friend who is brewing, so we take turns going in to the show."

Darwin brews stouts, ales, and lagers, all dubbed under the name "Evolution Ale." (His parents named him Darwin Adam.) Brewing since 1991, he loves experimenting with fruit and spiced beer and around Christmas time he makes spiced ale with ginger and allspice.

"I used to drink a lot of beer," he explains. "I actually used to drink more beer than I drink now. I just realized after a while that it would be a lot cheaper to make it. It's just the initial investment of buying the brewing equipment that really held me back. It's a lot cheaper and you can brew better beer, and whatever kind you want. I've been trying to get where I am totally self-sufficient. It's so much cheaper, and everything's better when you make it yourself. I just love it. I love beer."

So much so that he plans to use his business administration studies at Humboldt University in Arcata, California, to aid him in opening his own brew pub one day.

"That's what I'd like to do for a living," he says. "In this area it's so killer because there's a lot of micro-breweries, and that's a good start to working breweries. That's the ultimate goal. If I can end up in a situation like that, I'll be set forever. I'd just be so happy doing something I want to do."

He is enthusiastic about living in the Humboldt-county area, but getting to a show isn't as easy as when he lived in Oakland; it was a five-minute train ride to the Oakland Coliseum. Since the Dead don't play in Northern California much anymore, Darwin will have to settle for making the trek back down to Oakland.

"I'm going to have to commute, make the five- or six-hour drive back down to Oakland. That's the only reason I'm going to miss the Bay area, to see concerts and stuff. There's not too much up here for concerts."

He's committed because he loves the Dead as much as he did when he was a kid. He started listening when he was twelve and saw his first show at fourteen. By then he had boxes full of bootleg tapes.

"As long as I can remember I've liked the Dead. That's been my favorite band. When I was in high school, it was either reggae or the Grateful Dead, and there was no real in between. I'd go for a month just reggae, and then for the rest of the year just Grateful Dead."

Chocolate Stout

(servings: 2 to 2 1/2 cases of 12 oz. bottles)

This recipe cannot be made without the proper brewing equipment. If you don't have it, find a friend who does, and spend a day together brewing! These are beginner recipes, so it should be easy!

2 to 3 gallons of water, depending on the size of your pot, but 5 gallons will be used altogether

7.5 lbs. dark malt extract

1/2 lb. dark brown sugar

1/2 lb. bitter sweet non-dairy chocolate

1 lb. crystal malt

1/2 lb. black malt

1/2 lb. chocolate malt

1/3 lb. roasted barley

3 oz. fuggles hops (bittering)

6 tsps. gypsum

2 tsps. Irish moss

1 oz. Fuggles hops (finishing)

3/4 cup corn sugar (bottling)

1–2 pkg. ale yeast

Crack and crush the grains. Add the grains to a nylon grain bag, put in water, and let boil. Boil the bag for 1–3 minutes, then remove the bag. The reason to use the grains is for coloring and body.

Then add the rest of the ingredients to this water, add the sugars, chocolate, extract, bittering hops, gypsum. Boil 30–40 minutes.

Add Irish moss and boil for the remaining 10 minutes. During the last 2 to 4 minutes, add the finishing hops.

Fill the glass carboy up with 1/2 to 1 gallon cold water.

Sparge from brew pot to glass carboy.

Add yeast when cool and attach blow-off hose.

Bottle when fermentation is complete (about 2 weeks).

Remember: Always compost your spent grains and hops!

Cranberry Celebration Ale
(2 to 2 1/2 cases of 12 oz. bottles)

2 to 3 gallons of water, depending on the size of your pot
7 lbs. light malt extract
1/2 lb. crystal malt (cracked)
1 pkg. fresh cranberries (whole)
2 tsp. gypsum
1/8 lb. toasted malt
2 oz. northern brewer hops (bittering)
1/2 oz. cascade hops (finishing)
2 tsp. Irish moss
1–2 pkg. ale yeast

In a nylon bag, add the grains and then let come to a boil. Remove the grains when the boiling starts. Boil the extract, gypsum, bittering hops for 30 minutes.
Add Irish moss, boil for 10 minutes. The last 1–2 minutes, add cascade hops.
Sparge when cool and add yeast.
When initial fermentation is complete (blow-off stops), crush berries and add to glass fermenter. It is wise to use a 6–6 1/2 gallon carboy to leave room for the berries. Also, keep an eye on the fermentation airlock, berries may become stuck and unfriendly pressure may result in breakage. (Darwin had a cranberry explosion a few months back.)
Keg or bottle when complete.

Staying in one place for too long can make anyone want to hit the road and start a life in a new area. Steve Rogalski spent his adolescence growing up in Phoenix, Arizona, where his family has lived for years. Sick of living in the city, he decided to make a move to Prescott, a few hours north of Phoenix to live in, "the high, cool country."

Steve is in the process of building his house in the mountains of Prescott, on property that his family has owned for thirty-five years.

"I don't want to live up in the city where I grew up," he says. "My family had property up in Prescott, and that's where I want to live. I believe that I was conceived up there, and I kinda just feel really wonderful there. Safe. It's just that type of feeling.

"It's probably been twenty years I've been wanting to do it," he maintains. "I knew I wanted to get out of the regular thing after seven days into a vacation when I went mountain climbing. I was sitting in this one pasture, resting in the evening. All my friends had already taken off, because they were there for the weekend, and I just knew that I had to do something else, all by myself out there, watching the sun set."

Steve plans to construct his house in a dramatically different way than most houses are built today. He is actually building the house into the side of a mountain. By doing so, he wants to prove that you can live in a house that is ecologically safe.

"I want to live in an alternative-type house, a really nice one that will go into magazines. That people will see that you don't have to be on the grid, and you can build a house that's really comfortable to live in. Turn a lot of people onto solar, and composting toilets, and things like that.

"I'm digging down into the mountain and the whole top is going to be like a greenhouse," says Steve. "I'm just digging out around the big rocks that are in the mountain. The floors and walls will be rock. I'm a rock climber, so I'll be able to climb around my house when I want to. I'll build the house inside of it. Once the roof is finished, all the different floors and walk ways should be done in about a year or two.

"Part of the greenhouse will be heated, maybe with chickens," he explains. "I'm going to have a little creek running through the middle of the house, so when it rains it will fill a nice little water pool. Then I'll build wood floors, grow flowers and food inside of it. I'm hoping it will be like a greenhouse. During the winter, because it will have a glass roof, and all the rest is rock inside, the mass in the rock should hold the heat at night. I'm hoping just to have fun and do something different."

In the meantime, Steve tries to go to as many Dead shows that he finds time for, and at the scorching 1994 Las Vegas summer shows, he and his girlfriend Kery came to see the show, hang out, and sell "Banana Delight," a recipe he discovered while in Mexico.

"I learned how to make it last year in San Carlos, Mexico," he explains. "A funny thing happened. It tasted so wonderful and it made me feel so good, except the guy who made it used city water and by the time I got home, a day or so later, I had one day of hell."

At the shows, it was the first time Steve prepared the Banana Delight, and it sold well. "I'd rather see a lot more people drinking the banana drink, instead of the beer, and soda pop and stuff that dries you out," he says. "I wanted to make a go of it and see what would happen. But Kery is loving it, so she's probably going to start making it for herself. Something good that she can have that's easy to make."

"The Dead are good," explains Steve. "I can go sit there and dance through the whole show straight through and just have a great time, talk to people who aren't afraid to smile, and aren't afraid to be themselves, or at least be something."

Banana Delight
(serves 1)

3 bananas
1 cup raw brown rice or bottled brown rice syrup
1/4 cup honey
Cinnamon, to taste
Ice

Cook the brown rice down until it starts to become a syrup, a brown rice syrup. Add a little water to it now and then. Cook it down more and pour it through a strainer until it starts to make a syrup. The alternative to this process is to buy a bottle of brown rice syrup.
Blend up the bananas. Cook a little of the brown rice syrup and the bananas together. Melt in honey and mix well just before it's done cooking. Steve suggests that you don't cook the honey too much, or a lot of the minerals will be cooked out of it.
Pour over ice. "I made a concentrate of it, froze it up to travel, then just poured it off, added water and ice to it, mixed it all up," says Steve. He recommends mixing the drink now and then, for it will settle.

Clad in a long black coat and hat, Kym Trippsmith stands behind a black cloth that is thrown over her Volkswagen bus, as she steams water and milk. It is a makeshift curtain which conceals the fact that she is making espresso, cappuccino, caffe latte, killer mocha java, and Amazon Chai in the parking lot. On this Chinese New Year show run, the Oakland Coliseum parking lot security has been harsh. On days like this, many vendors complain about security closing down their operations or taking away merchandise. Kym is no exception.

Should she get shut down, she may have more at stake than many of the vendors in the lot. Taking her espresso-cappuccino maker to events enables her to raise money for Amazon Productions, a fundraising group that she founded in 1992. The non-profit organization orchestrates two benefits each year in effort to raise money for the Homeless of Marin County, and the Children's Sexual Abuse Treatment Programs, both of Marin County California. Kym began the group when she wanted to do something positive for the problems she saw around her.

"It came out of being tired of everyone just sitting around, going, 'Oh, yeah, it's all fucked up and I can't do anything about it.' So I decided that we would figure out a way to do something about it," she explains. "Last year we gave them about 2,500 dollars. Kids in Marin are on a three to six month waiting list to get any kind of

Amazon Chai
(serves 2)

According to Kym, Amazon Chai is a ginger tea blended with cardamom and spearmint. It is an Indian delight which is prepared without milk, but then the milk is added after it is steamed. She suggests sprinkling nutmeg, cinnamon, or grating fresh chocolate on top.

2 cups of water
2 pinches cardamom
2 handfuls of grated ginger
2 large spearmint leaves
Black decaffeinated tea, 2 teaspoons
Milk
Honey
Nutmeg, cinnamon, chocolate (optional)

Bring the water to a boil and pour it over the tea, cardamom, ginger, and spearmint leaves. Strain and add steamed milk. Include honey if desired.
Add nutmeg, cinnamon, or grated chocolate on top!

144

treatment, and that's one of the richest counties in the United States. It's unbelievable that you've got to get women together to put on benefits just to get the kids to the counseling sessions."

The group is primarily made up of women who want to contribute to their community, but haven't been given the opportunity or the cause. "We get together and offer them the ability to do it by putting on our benefits," she says. "We're just trying to inspire the Amazon spirit in both men and women around us," she adds.

The group raises money for the benefits by selling their wares at festivals, events, and sometimes Grateful Dead concerts. But as the day goes on at Oakland, security hassles grow and Kym becomes agitated when she cannot keep pumping out coffee to the small crowd that has gathered around the area.

"We find that it's a hassle to vend at Dead shows because they've been down on things," she says. "I think that the Grateful Dead should take more responsibility for the subculture that they created and focus it. There's a lot of energy out here. But they're abandoning what they created."

❀ Photo Credits ❀

• intro photo p. viii / *James Crossman* • intro photo p. xi / *E. Schoenfeld* • Tom (Fatty Eggrolls) / *Alec Bauer* • Rasananda (Samosas) / *Elizabeth Zipern* • Danbo (Falafel) / *Elizabeth Zipern* • Julia (# Bean Chili) / *Elizabeth Schoenfeld* • Tracey (Kabobs Made with Love) / *Raquel Heiny* • Lisa, Matt & Mike (Torchin' Hot Tuna Melts) / *Elizabeth Zipern* • Dean & Silvana (Guacamole and Salsa) / *Elizabeth Zipern* • Andre (Good Lovin' Lentil Soup) / *Alec Bauer* • Todd (9 Veggie Stir Fry) / *Elizabeth Schoenfeld* • Greg & Erin (The Gilly Melt) / *Raquel Heiny* • Tom, Coco, & Jean-Phillipe (Mesclun Wrap) / *Elizabeth Zipern* • Brayton (Vegan Sushi) / *Alec Bauer* • Lentil Lada / *Alec Bauer* • Stylin' Fat Veggie Pizza / *Alec Bauer* • Dave & Grizz (Fatty Fear Pizza) / *Elizabeth Zipern* • Harvest (Wheat Berry Pizza) / *Elizabeth Zipern* • Tara (Navajo Fried Bread) / *Alec Bauer* • Paul (Oatmeal Chocolate Chip Raisin Banana Cookie) / *James Crossman* • Feather (Karma Korn) / *Alec Bauer* • Teri (Banana Bread) / *Elizabeth Schoenfeld* • Theresa & Russ (Beautiful Breads) / *Elizabeth Zipern* • Bhakta (Energy Nuggets) / *Alec Bauer* • William & kids (Apple Space Cakes) / *Elizabeth Zipern* • Rachel & Dupree (Sesame Noodles) / *Elizabeth Zipern* • Matt & Kristin (Cold Sesame Noodles) / *Elizabeth Zipern* • Todd (Pesto Pasta) / *Elizabeth Schoenfeld* • Tim (Sumptuous Stir Fry) / *Stephanie Siebert* • Jeff (High Thai) / *Amelia Josey* • Jeff (Creation #68) / *Alec Bauer* • Brian (Fresh Hot Veggie Burger) / *Raquel Heiny* • Jim (Tofu Sandwich, Herbal REjuvenator) / *Raquel Heiny* • Heather & Tim (Veggie Pitas) / *Elizabeth Zipern* • Greg (Nature Burger) / *Elizabeth Schoenfeld* • Grilled Cheese on Honeywheat / *Alec Bauer* • Tim & Meredith (Kind Veggie Bagel) / *Raquel Heiny* • Mark (Grilled Cheese) / *Alec Bauer* • Amilius (Sprouted Organic Humous) / *Elizabeth Zipern* • James (Black Bean Burrito) / *Elizabeth Zipern* • Humous Tabouli Burrito / *Elizabeth Zipern* • Willow & Dragon (Rainbow Burritos) / *Mark Dabelstein* • Naomi (No-Cook Veggie Burritos) / *Mark Dabelstein* • Lionel & Jake (Good Karma Curry Burritos) / *Elizabeth Zipern* • Ken & friends (Stir Fry Burritos) / *Elizabeth Zipern* • The Flyin' Burrito Circus / *Alec Bauer* • Chris (Fruit Smoothie) / *Chris Kulina* • Kristen (Strawberry Lemonade) / *Elizabeth Zipern* • Matt & Kristina (Latte and Italian Soda) / *Elizabeth Zipern* • Matt & Kristina's bus / *Elizabeth Zipern* • Chris & Kyle (Psychedelic Fruit Bobs) / *Elizabeth Zipern* • Adam (Golden Devotion Potion) / *Elizabeth Schoenfeld* • Cosmis Coffee and Espresso / *Jonathan Edwards* • Kery & Steve (Banana Delight) / *James Crossman* • Darwin &Jennifer (Chocolate Stout) / *Alec Bauer* • Kym (Amazon Chai) / *Alec Bauer*